THE EFFECTS OF ENRICHMENT TUTORING UPON SELF-CONCEPT, EDUCATIONAL ACHIEVEMENT, AND MEASURED INTELLIGENCE OF MALE UNDERACHIEVERS IN AN INNER-CITY ELEMENTARY SCHOOL

BY: CLARENCE R. OLSEN

PALO ALTO, CALIFORNIA
1979

PUBLISHED BY

R & E RESEARCH ASSOCIATES, INC.
936 INDUSTRIAL AVENUE
PALO ALTO, CALIFORNIA 94303

PUBLISHERS

ROBERT D. REED AND ADAM S. ETEROVICH

Library of Congress Card Catalog Number
79-65268

I.S.B.N.
0-88247-588-6

81-10815
Copyright 1979
By
Clarence R. Olsen

ACKNOWLEDGEMENTS

Looking backward in an attempt to define those individuals who have been instrumental in the completion of this study is seemingly a very difficult, if not impossible, task. How does one acknowledge so many? The writer recognizes that the following acknowledgments perhaps do not include all those who have contributed to the study, but nevertheless he would like to extend his deepest gratitude:

To Dr. Clyde M. Campbell for trust and confidence in the writer's ability and without whose guidance the undertaking of the study would have been less likely.

To Dr. David C. Smith for his patience, guidance, and understanding manner in all matters pertinent to the study.

To Dr. James B. McKee and Dr. Troy L. Stearns.

To the Mott Foundation whose economic support enabled the writer to become involved in the study.

To the members of the staff of the Mott Institute for Community Improvement for the time, assistance, and never-ceasing encouragement rendered when needed and possible.

To the members of the community of the participating school district including: school administrators, teachers, pupils, parents, and volunteer enrichment tutors for their time, energy, and cooperation.

And finally to a loving and understanding family--which includes my wife and helpmate, Shirley, and our wonderful daughters: Nina, Dawn, and Cara--for waiting and waiting and waiting and waiting for the completion of Chapter V.

TABLE OF CONTENTS

LIST OF TABLES

CHAPTER 1

THE PROBLEM

Introductory Statement

One of the critical problems in education today concerns the planning of educational programs for male underachievers in the inner-city elementary school. Children of the inner city, both males and females, may achieve at lower levels than their counterparts who are located outside of the core of the city. Social class differences within and outside the school are often the conditions that result in underachievement. Martin Deutsch, an authority in the field of urban education, observed:

> Currently, 40 to 70 per cent of the total school population in our twenty largest cities consists of children from the most marginal economic and social circumstances. By the time these children reach junior high school, 60 per cent are retarded in reading by one to four years.[1]

The growth patterns of urban areas within the United States are conducive to the development of an underachieving population within the confines of the inner city. Urban areas tend to develop in concentric circles, with the older residents moving further from the center of the city as prosperity increases. New unskilled migrants move into the downtown and central areas. Such a pattern of movement results in people of similar income groups being clustered together within the city.[2] The inner-city population tends to be a stratified group of predominately unskilled or semi-skilled workers who have moved to the city from a rural region. The ethnic and racial composition tends to be primarily from the so-called minority groups--southern Negro, Puerto Rican, Appalachian white, American Indian, Mexican and most recently, Cuban.[3]

Sociologists argue that society is organized into different strata that are known roughly to its members. These strata are called social classes or socioeconomic levels. Various objective factors form the basis of assignment to any one class, among which are educational level, financial status, area of residence and length of residence in a community.[4] Sexton states:

> Family income is one index to social class, almost no matter how the term is defined. There are many other indices: occupation of father, type of housing, educational levels, etc. Family income is very highly correlated with all other indices. Thus a "lower-class" family will tend to have a low income, lower-status (and

lower paying) occupations, poor housing, and low educational levels. A family possessing any one of these
characteristics will tend to possess all of them.[5]

The inner city does indeed have its share of lower-class families,
but it also has a mass of working-class families who are either
satisfied with their situation or cannot move out of the inner
city. Ravitz[6] recognizes that there are other groups which are
not of an immigrant, low socioeconomic, or minority status whose
values resemble those of depressed urban dwellers and whose children do not achieve adequately.

Regardless of class status or race, the resident of the inner city, as a rule, is one who possesses a lower income. In addition, his educational achievement level is low, his home less
impressive than other homes, and his job generally classes among
those of low-status occupations.

Sexton's[7] account, Education and Income, clearly indicates
that achievement in the inner-city elementary school is below the
national average. Her findings with regard to Iowa Achievement
Test results in "Big City" show that: (1) Students in all schools
above the $7,000 family income level are achieving above grade
level at grades four and six while students in all schools below
the $7,000 family income level are achieving below grade level at
grades four and six. (2) In general, student achievement scores
tend to go up as income levels go up. (3) In the fourth grade,
the lowest level income group is achieving almost one whole year
below grade level. At the same time the highest level income
group is achieving more than one year above grade level. These
findings do not mean that the social class level of the individual family determines the achievement of the child. They do lend
support to the findings of the Coleman Report[8] that imply there
is a strong relationship between the social class composition of
the school and the educational attitudes and achievement of its
students.

Results from empirical evidence indicate that in the early
school years in the inner city, females on the average outperform
males in certain school subjects, especially reading. The findings in Deutsch's[9] recent study of 400 fourth, fifth, and sixth
grade low-income inner-city pupils that used an experimental
group of predominately Negro pupils and a control group of predominately white pupils to verify this. The evidence indicates
that within the control group, females outperformed males in
reading achievement and that within the experimental group, females achieved significantly better than males in all areas of
achievement. Regardless of race, females involved in this study
tend to exhibit more desirable achievement characteristics than
males.

Underachievement of male pupils in the inner-city elementary
school is a problem that must be confronted. The evidence implies that program development to meet the needs of these youngsters should be undertaken.

Background of the Problem

Underachievement among those less fortunate is a concern to the whole of the United States: federal, state, and local governments plus civic groups and private foundations are contributing vast sums of money, time, and effort in a concerted mobilization of resources for programs in areas where economic and social deprivation are factors determining achievement levels of children. Most of the programs presently underway can best be defined as compensatory educational programs. Gordon and Wilkerson comment:

> What all these programs and practices have in common is a dual goal—remedial work and prevention. They are remedial in that they attempt to fill gaps, whether social, cultural, or academic, in a child's total experience; they are preventative in that by doing so they aim to forestall either an initial or a continuing failure in school, and, by extension, in later life.[10]

The number and content of programs designed for compensatory purposes are ever increasing. When Gordon and Wilkerson developed their original study of compensatory education, the initial survey revealed programs in 108 communities, but more recent data indicate programs are being generated so rapidly that an accurate count is almost impossible. The contents of programs tend to be varied and may be classified under the following categories: teacher recruitment and training, curricular innovation, reading and language development, counseling and guidance, extra-curricular innovation, parental involvement and community involvement.[11]

Included among the various compensatory educational programs are many that use volunteer and paid teacher aides. These aides serve as tutors for academic and/or enrichment purposes, as resource personnel, counselors, home visitors representing the schools, leaders for study centers, and school and classroom aides in general.[12]

Many programs are organized for the express purpose of enrichment and/or academic tutoring. A recent survey of tasks performed by volunteer and paid teacher aides undertaken by the Educational Research Service points to the fact that tutoring individual students ranks fourth and fifteenth in a group of 25 tasks performed by volunteer and paid aides, respectively. Over half of the 217 systems reporting state that teacher aides are used in this capacity.[13]

Although tutors or enrichment tutors are not often defined as significant others, the qualities attributed to them by proponents of tutorial programs tend to classify them in this category. Many definitions of tutorial relationships imply that the tutor or enrichment tutor serves in the capacity of a friend or an "almost" relative. A definition of the tutoring role in a recent handbook for tutors states:

Tutoring is not teaching. Tutoring simply provides the assistance and support which a concerned parent can and often does provide. Experienced educators agree that those not trained for teaching can change a student's picture of himself and his attitude through effective tutoring.[14]

Carter,[15] writing with reference to a program involving retirees in the tutorial role, states: "The casual observer watching the seniors work might say they look like grandfathers counseling their grandchildren. In fact, this intimacy is encouraged and is a part of the picture." A volunteer coordinator's manual developed by the personnel directing this program, although not giving specific mention to the role of significant others, does note that the volunteer can often serve as a positive image when parents are absent from the home.[16]

Advocates[17, 18] of the tutorial program, academic and/or enrichment, emphasize that such programs enhance pupil self-concept and increase achievement levels of the participating pupils. They argue gains in self-concept and achievement are attributable to the pupils' participation in the tutorial program, yet to date there is little objective evidence to substantiate these claims.

The Educational Enrichment Program is one of a number of projects within the purview of the Mott Institute for Community Improvement of Michigan State University. The Mott Institute for Community Improvement, founded by the Charles Stewart Mott Foundation of Flint, Michigan, has as a basic objective the training of community school personnel to work in the inner-city setting.[19] The program is designed to use volunteer personnel from the community in the capacity of enrichment tutors.

The Director of the Mott Institute for Community Improvement, Dr. Clyde M. Campbell, foresees the program as one in which underachieving

> . . . young people under the age of ten will be removed from the classroom [once a week] for special care and attention. . . . A highly qualified person will see that these boys and girls are tested, interviewed, counseled and assigned to enrichment tutors for clinical treatment. Most of these enrichment tutors will be laymen with little, if any, professional preparation. How the para-professionals [enrichment tutors] function may depend on the needs of the youngsters.[20]

He recognizes that underachievers in the inner city are often saddled by the problem of a less than adequate self-image that results from social conditions as well as failure in schools and envisions the enrichment tutors assisting in the positive resolution of this problem by giving "warmth--kindness--love--and attention to these young people."[21]

The concern of this study is to determine the effectiveness

of enrichment tutoring. The data generated by the Educational Enrichment Program is the basis of this study.

Statement of Problem

There are two purposes for this exploratory study: The primary purpose is to analyze the effects of enrichment tutoring with male underachievers in the second, third, and fourth grades of an inner-city school upon (1) self-concept, (2) achievement, and (3) measured intelligence; a secondary purpose is to assess the effectiveness of the program as viewed by the participating teachers.

This study seeks to determine if inner-city underachieving pupils can be more effectively reached through enrichment tutoring in addition to the regular classroom procedure as opposed to regular classroom procedure alone. The theory underlying the study attempts to explain how changes can be effected through enrichment tutoring.

Theoretical Orientation

The theoretical orientation for this study evolves from the social psychology of Mead[22] as espoused by Brookover and Gottlieb,[23] the perceptual psychology of Snygg and Combs[24] and aspects of the helping relationship as developed by Rogers.[25]

Basically, it is argued that the self-concept develops as a product of experience and interaction with others in the social setting. Research by Brookover[26] and associates drawn from the interactionist theory indicates a positive relationship between self-concept and school achievement. Other evidence in the same research is supportive of the idea that pupil self-concept is related to the image the pupil perceives significant others hold of him. Significant others are defined by over- and underachieving students as parents, teachers, other school personnel and peers.[27]

A basic assumption of this study is that an enrichment tutor serves in the role of significant other in a helping relationship with underachievers. In the role of significant other the enrichment tutor is capable of influencing pupil self-concept and achievement.

Further basis for the theoretical orientation is established in Chapter II of this study.

Definition of Terms

For purposes of clarification, the following terms are defined:

Underachiever is defined as a pupil whom a classroom teacher defines as achieving below grade level and whose achievement, as measured by a composite score on the <u>California Achievement Test</u>, <u>1963 Revision</u>, is two months or more <u>below grade level</u> at the time of test administration. A pupil defined by the school district for placement in special education classes or classes for the emotionally disturbed is not included in the underachieving population. Farquhar and Payne, in a study of classification of achievement, state that one method of defining underachievement and overachievement is "by dichotomizing a distribution of combined aptitude and achievement measures."[28]

<u>Significant Other</u> is defined as a person whom the pupil "perceives to be important to him, and the reciprocal, to whom he as a pupil perceives himself to be important to."[29]

<u>Enrichment Tutor</u> is defined as a non-certificated person who volunteers his services to work with an assigned underachiever on a one-to-one basis. The enrichment tutor is involved in a "helping relationship" in the performance of his enrichment tutorial tasks. Using characteristics of the "helping relationship,"[30] the enrichment tutor exhibits empathy and warmth for the underachiever, is trustworthy in his relationships with the underachiever, and makes an effort to be cognizant of the innate potentialities of the underachiever.

<u>Tutorial Tasks</u> are defined as those tasks that involve the enrichment tutor and the underachiever in efforts to improve academic skills of the underachiever.

<u>Enrichment Tasks</u> are defined as those tasks that involve the enrichment tutor and the underachiever in field trips, social activities, games, conversation, and general counseling regarding school.

<u>Inner-City Elementary School</u> is defined as a school designated in an area the Board of Education names as an educationally depressed area, and which participates in one or both of the following programs: (a) Title I programs under the Elementary-Secondary Education Act, or (b) a special program designed for those schools which exhibit similar characteristics to those participating in (a), but who do not meet the guidelines for participation in (a).

<u>Self-Concept</u>, as defined by Combs, is the way in which an individual characteristically sees himself. This is the way he "feels" about himself.[31] In this study it is used to mean the way an individual perceives himself in his relationships with others, his school relationships and his social relationships. Self-concept is concerned with the total surroundings of the individual including people with whom he has contact and the environment in which he lives.

<u>Self-Report</u> is defined as the way an individual describes himself when he is asked to do so[32] and in this study refers to the reported self-concept as measured by the <u>Coopersmith Self-Esteem Inventory</u>.

Educational Achievement is defined as the level at which competency in educational skills is empirically demonstrated by test scores as converted to grade level equivalents. These levels are determined by performance on a group-administered standardized achievement test. The California Achievement Test, 1963 Revision, is the achievement test used in the study.

Measured Intelligence is defined as the score on an instrument purported to measure innate abilities as demonstrated by an intelligence quotient. The intelligence quotient is determined from the results on a standardized test scale. The California Short Form Test of Mental Maturity, 1963 Revision, is the test that was administered in this study.

The Hypotheses

Within this study one primary research hypothesis is investigated.

H_1 The reported self-concept scores of inner-city elementary school male underachievers who experience enrichment tutoring will be more positive than the scores of inner-city elementary school male underachievers who did not experience enrichment tutoring.

Two subsidiary hypothesis are also investigated since scores of educational achievement and measured intelligence are available.

H_2 The educational achievement scores of inner-city elementary school male underachievers who experience enrichment tutoring will be more positive than the scores of inner-city elementary school male underachievers who did not experience enrichment tutoring.

H_3 The measured intelligence scores of inner-city elementary school male underachievers who experience enrichment tutoring will be more positive than the scores of inner-city elementary school male underachievers who did not experience enrichment tutoring.

Assumptions

In this study it is assumed:

1. A significant number of inner-city elementary school males are not achieving commensurate with their ability.

2. Underachieving behavior is amenable to change.

3. Self-concept is amenable to change.

4. A self-report instrument measures self-concept.

7

5. At the time the various instruments are administered, the attitudes, achievement, and measured intelligence are accurately measured.

6. Uncontrolled variables--age, social-economic status, skill of enrichment tutors, family background-- distribute their effects randomly throughout the experimental and control groups.

7. Enrichment tutors can become significant others.

8. It is valuable to know if enrichment tutoring is an effective method of changing self-concept, achievement, and measured intelligence.

Limitations of the Study

Generalizations to be drawn from this study are limited to second, third, and fourth grade male pupils from the inner city of a midwestern industrial city with a population of approximately 200,000.

The school used for the study is one of 14 classified as inner-city schools by the participating school district. The population of the school is majority Negro as is the population of underachievers from which the experimental and control groups are drawn.

Sample size is another limiting factor of this study. Although both the experimental and control groups are composed of 30 members or more, tests of significance are calculated by grade level, and the size of the groups per grade level is considerably less than that number. The tests of significance that are used are those designed for the study of small samples that result in greater calculation for error.

The Coopersmith Self-Esteem Inventory, the general self-concept instrument used in this study, is an instrument that is acceptable to the participating school district and is frequently used to measure the self-concept of elementary pupils. There are questions relating to the measure of a general self-concept as opposed to a specific self-concept when the problem is of an educational nature.[33] In addition some authorities question the use of self-report instruments to measure self-concept.[34]

Lastly, the assumption that an enrichment tutor can become a significant other is a possible limiting factor. Research indicates school personnel may or may not become significant others.[35] It is possible that some pupils may not benefit from the relationship.

Organization of the Study

The general format of the study is as follows: In Chapter II a review of the literature relating to self-concept, achievement and measured intelligence change is undertaken. The design of the study which includes sampling procedures, method of treatment, statistical hypotheses, and method of analysis represents the content of Chapter III. The results of the analysis are reported in Chapter IV. In Chapter V, the summary, conclusions and implications for future research are presented.

[1]Martin Deutsch, "Nursery Education: The Influence of Special Programming on Early Development," *The Disadvantaged Child*, ed. Martin Deutsch (New York: Basic Books, Inc., 1967), p. 77.

[2]Patricia C. Sexton, *Education and Income* (New York: Viking Press, 1961), p. 4.

[3]A. Harry Passow, "Schools in Depressed Areas," *Education in Depressed Areas*, ed. A. Harry Passow (New York: Teachers College, Columbia University, 1963), pp. 1-2.

[4]Joan I. Roberts, "General Introduction," *School Children in the Urban Slum*, ed. Joan I. Roberts (New York: The Free Press, 1967), p. 7.

[5]Sexton, *op. cit.*, p. 11.

[6]Mel Ravitz, "The Role of the School in the Urban Setting," *Education in Depressed Areas*, ed. A. Harry Passow (New York: Teachers College, Columbia University, 1963), pp. 6-23.

[7]Sexton, *op. cit.*, pp. 23-136.

[8]James S. Coleman *et al.*, *Equality of Educational Opportunity* (Washington, D. C.: U. S. Office of Education, Government Printing Office, 1966), p. 304.

[9]Martin Deutsch, "Minority Groups and Class Status as Related to Social and Personality Factors in Scholastic Achievement," *The Disadvantaged Child*, ed. Martin Deutsch (New York: Basic Books, Inc., 1967), pp. 108-109.

[10]Edmund W. Gordon and Doxey A. Wilkerson, *Compensatory Programs for the Disadvantaged* (New York: College Entrance Examination Board, 1966), p. 34.

[11]*Ibid.*, p. 31.

[12]*Ibid.*, pp. 54-122.

[13]National Education Association, Research Division and American Association of School Administrators, *Teacher Aides in Large School Systems: Educational Research Service Circular No. 2, 1967* (Washington, D. C.: National Education Association, April, 1967), p. 4.

[14]Office of Director of Community Schools, New Haven, Connecticut, "Handbook for Tutors," (Mimeographed Handbook, New Haven Public Schools, New Haven, Connecticut, 1967), p. 3.

[15]Howard A. Carter, "The Retired Senior Citizen as a Resource to Minimize Underachievement of Children in Public Schools," *Ar-*

chives of Physical Medicine and Rehabilitation, Vol. 35 (1964), pp. 218-223.

[16]Janet Freund, *Coordinator Guide* (Winnetka, Illinois: Winnetka Public Schools, 1966), pp. 71-83.

[17]Office of Director of Community Schools, New Haven, Connecticut, *loc. cit.*

[18]Gayle Janowitz, *Helping Hands* (Chicago: University of Chicago Press, 1965), pp. 87-118.

[19]Mott Institute for Community Improvement, "Presentation to Trustees," unpublished presentation to the Trustees of the Mott Foundation, March 1, 1968.

[20]Clyde M. Campbell, "The Educative Community," *The Community School and Its Administration*, 5 (1967), p. 3.

[21]*Ibid.*

[22]George H. Mead, *Mind, Self and Society* (Chicago: The University of Chicago Press, 1934).

[23]Wilbur B. Brookover and David Gottlieb, *A Sociology of Education* (New York: American Book Company, 1964).

[24]Donald Snygg and Arthur W. Combs, *Individual Behavior* (New York: Harper and Row, Publishers, 1959).

[25]Carl Rogers, *On Becoming a Person* (Boston: Houghton Mifflin Company, 1961), pp. 39-57.

[26]Wilbur Brookover, Ann Patterson, and Shailer Thomas, *Self-Concept of Ability and School Achievement* (East Lansing, Michigan: Office of Research and Publications, Michigan State University, 1962), p. 38.

[27]*Ibid.*, p. 57.

[28]William W. Farquhar and David A. Payne, "A Classification of Techniques Used in Selecting Under- and Overachieving Students," *American Personnel and Guidance Journal*, 42 (1964), pp. 874-884.

[29]Wilbur Brookover, Lepere, *et al.*, *Self-Concept of Ability and School Achievement*, II (East Lansing, Michigan: Office of Research and Publications, Michigan State University, 1965), p. 15.

[30]Rogers, *loc. cit.*

[31]Arthur W. Combs, "A Perceptual View of the Adequate Personality," *Perceiving, Behaving, Becoming*, ed. Arthur W. Combs (Washington, D. C.: Association for Supervision and Curriculum Development, National Education Association, 1966), p. 51.

[32]*Ibid.*

[33]Wilbur Brookover, Edsel L. Erickson, and Lee M. Joiner, *Self-Concept of Ability and School Achievement, III* (East Lansing, Michigan: Office of Research and Publication, Michigan State University, 1967), p. 145.

[34]Combs, *loc. cit.*

[35]Brookover, Patterson, *et al.*, *loc. cit.*

CHAPTER 2

REVIEW OF THE LITERATURE

The conceptualization of enrichment tutoring for the purposes of this study establishes a new construct. In recent years some educators have given consideration to the characteristics of such a construct, but very little seems to have been done to develop programs incorporating it.

In the literature there are indications that significant others influence the development of the individual's self-concept and educational achievement. The findings from research imply there are characteristics common to a positive helping relationship in teaching and counseling.

Some tutorial programs are designed to incorporate characteristics of the helping relationships. Other programs are under way that imply the role of significant others for the participating tutors. Although a number of investigations incorporate elements of enrichment tutoring, most studies are concerned with tutoring as it is traditionally defined. Nevertheless, the investigations of traditional and other tutorial programs are relevant for this study.

For the purpose of this review, literature relating the theoretical bases for self-concept development and empirical research studies, closely related to the problems of this study, are considered. The review of literature is categorized as follows:

1. Social nature of self-concept
2. Stability of self-concept
3. Measurement of self-concept
4. Relationship of self-concept and educational achievement
5. Negro self-concept
6. Significant others and self-concept
7. Helping relationships
8. Findings from tutorial programs

Social Nature of Self-Concept

Contemporary self-theory was founded in the psychology of William James.[1] In a definition of the total self, he acknowledged a two-faceted self, the "self as known" and the "self as knower." The "self as known" or a man's "Me" he defined as "the sum total of all that a man can call his, not only his body and his psychic powers, but his clothes and his house, his wife and children, his ancestors and friends, his reputation and works, his land and horses, and yacht and bank account."[2] The "self as knower" James called man's "I" and defined as "that which at any given moment is conscious, whereas the "Me" is only one of the things which it is conscious of."[3]

According to James the "self as known" had three components: "the material me," "the social me" and "the spiritual me." He argued that man has as many social self-images as there are individuals who recognize him and carry an image of him in their minds. In order for a social self to develop, James thought the individual must care about the concerned groups' opinions of himself.[4]

Since the work of James, theorists have presented additional arguments that have resulted in variations in theories of self. Wylie[5] categorized self theories into two classifications. The first classification, the phenomenological theory of self, emphasized the role of the conscious self. A second, based on non-phenomenal constructs, implied that an unconscious self influences human behavior. Theories of most perceptual theorists, with few exceptions, have fallen within the phenomenological school.

For the purposes of this study only the followers of the phenomenological school and theory of self as developed by the social psychologists have been considered. These theories seem to have gained acceptance in educational circles over the past 30 years.

Language was an essential part of the self theory as developed by Mead.[6] For his purposes, language was defined as reading meaning into the conduct of other people. Each person, he reasoned, arbitrarily defines a set of language symbols that must be learned by others in order for them to react to him. His definition of language was extended to encompass the conversation of gestures that included vocal gestures, physical gestures, body postures and other methods of non-verbal communication.

Since Mead felt the self originated in the process of social experience and activity, language was necessary for its development. Self, he believed, developed in the given individual as a result of his relation to the process of social experience as a whole and to the other individuals in the process. Mead described the evolvement of self-consciousness or self-awareness as being

> . . . definitely organized about the social individual, and that . . . is not simply because one is in a social group and affected by others and affects them, but because his own experience as a self is one which he takes over from his actions upon others. He becomes a self insofar as he can take the attitude of another and act toward himself as others act. Insofar as the conversation of gestures can become a part of conduct in the direction and control of experience, then a self can arise. It is the social process of influencing others in a social act and then taking the attitudes of others aroused by the stimulus and then in turn acting to this

response which constitutes a self.[7]

Jersild[8] detailed a self made up of all that goes into a person's experience in his individual existence. For him the self was the "composite of a person's thoughts and feelings, strivings and hopes, fears and fantasies, his view of what he is, what he has been, what he might become, and his attitudes pertaining to his worth." According to his logic the self possessed three components: the way a person perceives himself; his conception of his distinctive characteristics and attitudinal components that includes his feeling about himself; his attitudes about his present and future prospects and his attitudes of self-esteem and self-reproach. Jersild felt interpersonal relationships were among the earliest and most influential determinants of the individual's view of self.[9]

Snygg and Combs[10] in the phenomenological development of self postulated the existence of a perceptual field that included all of the individual's perceptions. These perceptions encompassed those things about himself and those things quite outside of himself, the not self. The phenomenal self was defined as all perceptions of self in a particular situation irrespective of importance to the individual. Snygg and Combs viewed the development of the phenomenal self in the following manner:

> As the child grows and explores himself, he discovers he is male or female, tall or short, fat or thin, blond or brunette. Some of these perceptions he arrives at through his own explorations of self. Other concepts, particularly those which have to do with values, he acquires from his interactions with people about him. He discovers not only what he is, but also what he is not and attaches values to these discriminations. He perceives himself as "good" or "bad," adequate or inadequate, handsome or ugly, acceptable or unacceptable, depending upon the ways he is treated by those who surround him in the growing-up years. He learns about himself not just from his own explorations, but through the mirror of himself represented by the actions of those about him.
>   The self is essentially a social product arising out of experience with people. Although some of the individual's experience of self may be achieved in isolation from other people, by far the greater portion arises out of his relationships with others. Human personality is primarily a product of social interaction. We learn the most significant and fundamental facts about ourselves from what Sullivan called "reflected appraisals," inferences about ourselves made as a consequence of the ways we perceive others behaving toward us. We learn who we are and what we are from the way we are treated by those who surround us; in our earliest years by our families, and in later years by all those people with whom we come in contact.[11]

They further differentiated the perceptual field to include those perceptions about self which seem most vital or important to the individual himself. The organization of these central perceptions of self was defined as the self-concept.[12]

Rogers[13] has been another major contributor to the phenomenological theory. In his development of personality theory, Rogers evolved a set of propositions that placed the self-concept in a position of control. The propositions have led him to a thesis of personality that is based on two primary elements. One element, experience, included the immediate field of sensory and visceral experience. For Rogers this element represented all that is experienced in the phenomenal field of the individual. The second element, the self-structure, according to Rogers arose in the following manner:

> As a result of interaction with the environment, and particularly as a result of evaluational interaction with others, the structure of self is formed--an organized, fluid, but consistent conceptual pattern of perceptions of characteristics and relationships of the "I" or the "me," together with values attached to these concepts.
> The values attached to experiences, and the values which are a part of the self-structure, in some instances are values experienced by the organism, and in some instances are values introjected or taken over from others, but perceived in distorted fashion, as if they had been experienced directly.[14]

Rogers viewed the self-structure, which he used synonymously with self-concept, as the primary element in personality. He argued that a configuration of self will sometimes conflict with experience. When this occurs, the configuration of self admitted to awareness represents a portion of the phenomenal field in which social or other experience has been distorted in symbolization and perceived as a part of the individual's own experience. Awareness, he believed, is denied to those sensory and visceral experiences at odds with the self-structure.[15]

Ideally, Rogers saw the end point of personality development as being a basic congruence between the phenomenal field of experience and the self-structure. He further argued that lack of congruence resulted in internal strain and anxiety in the individual. Client-centered therapy resulted from Rogers' efforts to determine a method to effect such congruence.[16]

Ausubel focused on the ego in the development of a theory of personality. He saw the ego as "the resultant of a process of continuous interaction between current social experience and the existing personality structure that is mediated by perceptual responses."[17] The self and the self-concept were constructs basic to Ausubel's definition of ego. He defined the self as "a constellation of individual perceptions and memories consisting of the visual image of the appearance of one's body, the auditory image of the sound of one's name, images of kinesthetic sensations and visceral tension, memories of personal events, etc." Self-concept, on the other hand, he defined as "an abstraction of the distinguishing characteristics of the self that differentiate an individual's 'selfhood' from the environment and other selves."[18]

Raimy stated "the self-concept is the map which each person consults in order to understand himself, especially during moments of crisis or choice."[19] He viewed the self-concept as more or less the organized perceptual object resulting from present and past self-observations in biological, social and historical settings.

Proponents[20] of the social-psychological view of self have based their arguments in the Meadian view. They have stated that their theoretical orientation is not incompatible with the phenomenological theories of self. Divergence of opinion has arisen only in regard to the origin of self. The phenomenologists have been primarily concerned with the individual, while the social psychologists have concerned themselves with the social situation in which the individual behaves. They have argued, "Recognition of social groups and the patterns of interaction in which the child is socialized and through which he learns the expected patterns of behavior provides the background for understanding the origin of the self-concept."[21] As a part of extensive research, Brookover and associates have defined self-concept as "symbolic behavior in which the individual articulates a program of action for himself as an object in relation to others."[22]

Stability of Self-Concept

Once a personality has been established in a given individual, the self-concept has a high degree of stability. The amount of change that is permitted to occur in self-concept over a period of time is dependent upon the individual and his internal view of a given situation.

Lecky[23] has postulated that the individual has been placed in an environment which he cannot understand. The individual, as a result, has been forced to create a substitute world which he can understand and in which he can place faith. He acts in consistency with the conception, derives his standards of value from it, and undertakes to alter it only when convinced by experience that it fails to serve his goals of unity. This self scheme of life is his only guarantee of security and its preservation becomes a life goal. Lecky has defined this process as "self consistency."

Snygg and Combs argued that "the phenomenal self with the self-concept at its core represents our fundamental frame of reference, our anchor to reality; and even an unsatisfactory self-organization is likely to prove highly stable and resistant to change."[24] Even with this statement they recognized that the phenomenal self is capable of change. For them change in self depended upon: (1) How important the new concept became to the individual's self-organization; (2) The relation of the new concept to the individual's basic need of maintenance and enhancement of self; and (3) The clarity of the perception of a new experience.[25]

For Rogers[26] the self-concept was a fluid but consistent organization which did not permit the intrusion of a perception at variance with it. According to Rogers any experience inconsistent with the organization of self may be perceived as a threat. He posited that the more perceptions of this nature there are, the more rigidly the self-structure is organized to maintain itself. Yet under conditions that involve an absence of threat to the self-structure, he argued revisions of self-concept including experiences inconsistent with it are possible.

Several research studies have been undertaken to study the stability of self-concept. In a study of self-esteem, Rosenberg[27] investigated the attitudes of 5,024 juniors and seniors in the public high schools of New York State. He designed and administered a set of self-esteem scales that included a self-esteem subscale and a stability of self subscale.

An analysis of the data indicated that the least stability of self was found among those who have rather low self-esteem. In other words, those who were found to hold negative opinions of themselves, seem to have the most changeable pictures of self. In addition, pupils with low self-esteem were much more likely than those with high self-esteem to have unstable self-conceptions. At the extremes, students with high self-esteem were three and one-half times as likely as those with low self-esteem to have "very stable" self pictures and the latter were four times as likely as the former to possess "very unstable" pictures of self.[28]

In a study involving 172 high school students, Engel[29] investigated the stability of self-concept over a two-year period. Tests were administered to a group of boys and girls in the eighth and tenth grades and again in the tenth and twelfth grades. A self-concept Q-sort consisting of items relevant to adolescent concerns was administered.

Engel hypothesized that the self-concepts of adolescents would be relatively stable over the two-year period. Stability was defined as relatively high correlations between the Q-sorts for the two administrations. An overall mean correlation of .53 was calculated. Although this represented a positive correlation, it did not indicate a high degree of stability. A second hypothesis predicted that the self-concepts of students with a positive attitude toward themselves on the first test would be significantly more stable over the two-year period than the self-concepts of students with a negative or defensive self-concept. The data indicated that students whose self-concepts were negative at the first testing were significantly less stable in self-concepts than students whose self-concepts were positive.[30]

Self-concept stability was of concern to Ketcham and Morse[31] in a recent study of the dimensions of children's social and psychological development related to school achievement. Two self-concept measures were taken for the purposes of the study. One measure, the Osgood Semantic Differential, was purported to measure pupil self-concept. A second, the Coopersmith Self-Esteem Inventory, related four scores of self-concept. The total scale gave a total self-measure while three subscales were designed to measure personal self, social self and school self. The instruments were administered to a stratified random sample of 430 pupils in the third, fourth, fifth, seventh, eighth and ninth grades during 1962 and again in 1963 and 1964.

The t-test was used to test the level of significance. Results from the Osgood Semantic Differential indicated a significant negative trend in self-concept for the original seventh-, eighth-, and ninth-grade groups over the total period (p = .05). The total scores from the Coopersmith Self-Esteem Inventory indicated a positive significant self-concept change for the fourth-grade group over the two-year period (p = .05). At the third- and fourth-grade levels there were positive significant gains in the area of social self for the period measured (p = .05). Negative significant gains were exhibited for school self at the fourth-, fifth-, seventh-, eighth-, and ninth-grade levels over the two-year time period (p = .05). When the researchers considered only the constant members of the class, more negative gains became apparent. They concluded, "As children progress through elementary and secondary grades, their self-image and self-esteem take on an increasingly negative quality."[32]

Measurement of Self-Concept

There has been considerable debate among researchers with regard to the measurement of self-concept. Several reviews[33, 34] of the literature have discussed information regarding self-concept instruments.

Gordon[35] has classified self-concept measurement into three broad categories: (1) self report; (2) inference based on observation of behavior; and (3) inference based on projective techniques. In Wylie's[36] review, measures were placed into two general classifications: phenomenological and nonphenomenological. Super[37] has described the three basic methods of personality assessment as: (1) the observation approach; (2) personality projection; and (3) self-description. Gordon's latter two categories, Wylie's nonphenomenological classification and Super's first two divisions of instruments represented methods designed for an observer to assess meaning from an external point of view. The self-report of Gordon, the phenomenological measures of Wylie and the self-description of Super represent classifications of instruments designed to assess self-concept from the internal point of view.

Most self-report instruments have been constructed on the assumption that individual differences exist in an overall or global self-evaluative attitude. Wylie has listed self-report instruments into the general areas of: (1) Q-sorts and (2) rating scales, questionnaires and adjective check lists.[38]

The Q-sort was developed by Stephenson[39] and has been used in numerous studies of self-concept. In the typical application of this technique the subject is instructed to sort a large number of personality-descriptive items into nine piles according to the degree they are characteristic of him. The subject is told to place specified numbers of items in each pile so as to yield a near normal distribution of items. He is then asked to perform a similar distribution according to his ideal self. Each item is then assigned a value from one to nine, according to the pile in which it is placed. Scores are tabulated for the subject's self-description and ideal self. A correlation coefficient is computed and self-regard is inferred from the magnitude of the correlation.

Rating scales, questionnaires and adjective checklists have been the most frequently used measures of self-concept. Most of these instruments, like the Q-sort, have been designed to measure self-regard. Wylie[40] has defined four categories of these instruments: (1) those which purport to measure self-regard directly; (2) those which use this direct approach and also derive a discrepancy score between self and ideal ratings; (3) those which utilize mainly a self-minus-ideal discrepancy score; and (4) those which rely on the subject's reports of actual self only, with the ideal end of the scale being assumed by the experimenter, or the favorability of the terms being defined in terms of external judges' opinions of desirability. These instruments have been designed to force the subject to decide for himself the situations to which the items refer. Usually the items have been defined in terms of extremes. Some instruments call for a simple "yes" or "no" answer while others demand that the subject place himself on a scale with reference to the extremities. Likert[41] introduced a technique of summated ratings in which the various alternatives for each item are assigned weights. Five categories are generally defined ranging from one to five points in value. The more favorable a person's attitude, the higher the score for the item.

Wylie[42] has cautioned that results obtained from self-report instruments are questionable and that those who utilize them should be concerned with construct validity. She proposed that the subjects' self-report responses are influenced by:

> (a) the subject's intent to select what he wishes to reveal to the experimenter; (b) the subject's intent to say that he has attitudes or perceptions which he does not have; (c) the subject's response habits; particularly those of introspection and the use of language; and (d) a host of situational and methodological factors which may not only induce variations in (a), (b), and (c), but may exert other more superficial influences on the responses obtained.[43]

Wylie has not been alone in her concern with regard to self-report instruments. Combs has cautioned that self-concept and self-report ". . . are by no means identical. What a person says he is and what he believes he is may be very far apart."[44]

In considering a research approach to therapy Rogers[45] suggested that the attitude measures and Q-sort techniques available are proper instruments for that purpose. Super[46] recognized that many of the instruments presently in use are valid self-descriptive devices. He stated that two approaches have been utilized to develop these instruments. The first, "the group difference method," consists of starting with a well-defined group, and developing a theoretical model that acts as a guide in item construction. The second, "the generalized model method," begins with a theory as to the significant dimensions of personality from which items are written and selected. He added that many of the adjective checklists and inventories developed since World War II have been developed along these lines and appear to offer promising results.

Relationship of Self-Concept and Educational Achievement

Learning has been defined in many ways. To John Dewey[47] learning suggested an antithesis in that he felt it could be defined in two ways. In one definition he viewed learning as the sum of what is known, that is, all that is handed down by learned men and books. Study he saw as a process by which an individual draws on what is known. In the second definition, learning meant something which the individual does when he studies. Dewey saw a dualism existing between knowledge as something external or objective as opposed to knowing something internal or subjective. For him the first definition was concerned with the part of life which is dependent upon a knowledge base and the latter represented that in which individuals are freer.

Hilgard[48] noted that many people are inclined to define learning as improvement with practice, or as profiting by experience, but he countered that some learning is not improvement nor for that matter is all learning desirable. To describe it as any change accompanying repetition, he argued, is to confuse it with growth, fatigue and other changes which may take place with repetition. He defined learning as:

> . . . the process by which an activity originates or
> is changed through reacting to an encountered situa-
> tion, provided that the characteristics of the change
> in activity cannot be explained on the basis of native
> response tendencies, maturation, or temporary states
> of the organism (e.g., fatigue, drugs, etc.).[49]

Cronbach[50] formulated a definition of learning that might be acceptable to most of those involved in education. He argued that if a person makes a different response this month than he made a month ago, he has learned something. Learning, he felt, is shown by a change in behavior as a result of experience and is exhibited when the same responses occur with increased frequency in a repeated situation. Formally he defined learning as "the modification of behavior through activity and experience which improves modes of adjustment to the environment."[51]

Travers[52] made a distinction between learning and performance. For him performance represented the observable behavior of the individual. Performance was the individual's response and if the response was modified over a period of time, learning had occurred. He argued that scientists have developed precise tools for the measurement of performance which take the form of the standardized achievement tests that have been accepted in the schools for the purpose of providing improved control over the learning process.

According to Chauncey and Dobbin[53] the achievement test has been designed to determine whether the student has learned what the teacher has been trying to teach him. Sometimes the achievement test has aimed at demonstrating increments of learning, while at other times it has been designed to cover a great deal of learning or complex behavior patterns. In every case the achievement test has been designed to provide a demonstration of learning.

Bernard[54] proposed that achievement tests are used to measure status in terms of subject matter. To him the most effective use of these tests involve the administration of pre- and post-tests to measure growth over a period of time.

Learning in the schools has been most often measured by academic achievement. Generally academic achievement has been determined by the yearly progress of children to the next higher grade or by their achievement test results.

In recent years concerned educators, psychologists and social scientists have investigated the correlation between self-concept and academic achievement. A positive relationship does appear to exist between the two variables. To date there has been little evidence to indicate a causal relationship, that is, does the development of the self-concept precede the degree of achievement or vice-versa. Several authorities[55, 56] have spoken to this bifurcation which has been delineated by Travers in the following manner:

> . . . the statement is commonly made that a person who thinks of himself as stupid is more likely to be poorly motivated in an academic learning situation than a person who thinks of himself as bright. The assumption underlying such a position is that there is a causal relation between the self-concept and the rate of learning, though the alternative is possible--that high achievement may produce a positive and constructive concept of self.[57]

A study of high school students undertaken by Schulman[58] sought to assess changes in self-estimates of ability from the ninth to the twelfth grade. In order to do this he compared self-estimates of ability with performances on objective ability tests. He found the congruence between the two to be greater for seniors than for freshmen. From this he concluded that students use educational experience to revise their self-picture. McDavid[59] hypothesized that high achievers have higher self-evaluations than low achievers. He found this to hold true for a sample of boys and suggested that this dimension of self-concept may operate as a feedback mechanism. In essence, he felt high academic performance may result in higher self-evaluation, which in turn may increase the motivation for attaining high grades in the future.

There are numerous studies which indicate a relationship between self-concept and achievement at the secondary and elementary school levels. In 1962 Gordon summarized the literature regarding this relationship and stated, "Thus, from studies of both high and underachievers the relationship between self-concept and achievement becomes clearer. There is a relationship between positive self-concept and high achievement; negative self-concept and underachievement."[60]

One of the most comprehensive studies of this nature was undertaken by a series of research teams headed by Brookover.[61] These teams investigated the relationships between self-concept of ability and academic achievement for a sample of 1,050 Caucasian boys and girls from an urban school system. The longitudinal study which spanned six years tested the hypothesis, "self-concept of ability in school is significantly and positively related to the academic performance of students even with an ability dimension controlled." The index of academic performance used was student grade-point average. The findings of the study showed the correlation between self-concept of ability and grade-point average to range from .48 to .63 over the six-year period. The only correlation to fall below .50 was for boys at the twelfth-grade level. An analysis of the achievement of students with high and low self-concepts of ability revealed that, although a significant proportion of students with high self-concepts of ability achieved at a relatively lower level, practically none of the students with lower self-concepts of ability achieved at a high level.

For the purpose of studying the relationship between self-concept and achievement, Fink[62] identified achievers and underachievers by grade-point average. The 84 boys and girls, who were members of a freshman class of a rural California high school, were matched according to I.Q. and sex. Several self-concept measures were administered to them. Total self-concept scores indicated positive relationships between self-concept and achievement. Chi-square tests showed the relationship for boys was significant at the .01 level while it was significant at the .10 level for girls.

In a study undertaken by Shaw, Edson and Bell,[63] the Sarbin Adjective Checklist was used to compare the self-concepts of achieving and underachieving groups of high school students. The checklist contained 200 adjectives indicative of positive and negative self-concept traits. The achievers exhibited a more positive attitude toward self by checking more often than under-achieving students the items associated with a positive self.

Several studies have sought to establish a relationship between educational achievement and self-concept at the elementary school level. This research has been concentrated at the upper levels of the elementary schools. A majority of the research has implied a positive relationship between the two variables.

Coopersmith[64] developed an inventory of self-esteem in order to explore the existing relationships between self-esteem and academic and social success and failure. His subjects consisted of 102 fifth- and sixth-grade boys and girls drawn from the public schools of a small Eastern city. In addition to the results for this instrument, Iowa Achievement Test results were obtained for each child from the school records. Sociometric data were obtained by asking the children in each of the four classes to indicate which three children in their class they would most like to have as their friends. This information was compiled on the total number of times each child was chosen by his classmates. The scores on the achievement test and sociogram were used as indices of success experiences. The data were subjected to correlational and chi-square analyses. The chi-square analysis showed a significant tendency (p = .05) for students above and below their class medians in self-esteem. Significant correlations were obtained between self-esteem and sociometric choice (r = .37, p = .01).[65]

Bodwin[66] investigated the relationship between an immature self-concept and certain educational disabilities. His research group consisted of 300 third- and sixth-grade boys and girls. Each was administered the Machover Draw A Person Test and an achievement test. He found that positive and very significant relationships existed between an immature self-concept and reading achievement and arithmetic achievement. The correlations obtained between self-concept and reading achievement were .72 at the third-grade level and .62 at the sixth-grade level. For arithmetic achievement and self-concept correlations of .78 at the third-grade level and .68 at the sixth-grade level were determined. The correlation between immature self-concept and median achievement test scores was .60.

Campbell[67] administered measures of academic achievement and self-concept to 158 fourth-, fifth-, and sixth-grade pupils in order to determine relationships between these variables. The data supported the hypothesis that there is a direct, linear relationship between self-concept and school achievement at these levels. According to the data, the relationship between self-concept and achievement was more pronounced for boys than for girls.

Bruck[68] reported positive and significant correlations between self-concepts and grade-point averages for a group of 300 third-, sixth- and eleventh-grade boys and girls (p = .05). In a study of 144 sixth-grade boys by Hayes,[69] significant correlations were indicated for a general self-concept of ability scale and arithmetic achievement (r = .48), teacher-assigned grades (r = .61) and total grade-point average (r = .67).

The results of some studies have indicated little relationship between self-concept and academic achievement. Butcher's[70] data for a sample of 120 pupils from third-, fourth-, fifth- and sixth-grade classes in six high-achieving schools led him to conclude he could not fully accept a hypothesis to that effect. An analysis of the data indicated significant correlations (p = .05) of .37 and .38 between self-concept and achievement at the fourth- and fifth-grade levels, respectively. However, he found correlations of .10 and -.04 at the third- and fourth-grade levels, respectively, which led to his conclusion.

Seymore[71] investigated the relationship between self-concept and academic success at the college level. Instruments were designed to measure role-concept and self-concept. Agreement between the students' self-picture and their successful student picture was not found to be significantly related to grades.

Negro Self-Concept

Although little empirical research has been undertaken with respect to the Negro self-concept in recent years, the topic was given considerable exposure before and during the Brown Versus Board of Education of Topeka decision[72] by the United States Supreme Court in 1954. This decision set the stage for the current thought regarding the Negro self-concept.

As early as 1947, results from an investigation performed by Kenneth and Mamie Clark[73] indicated racial recognition ability did not necessarily determine accurate racial self-identification. They found that in a group of Negro children 90 per cent could tell a Negro doll from a white one. Yet, among the same group, only 66 per cent could make correct self-identification with Negro dolls. In similar research reported by Trager and Yarrow,[74] both Negro and white children were found to value the white race more highly than the Negro race. When asked the question whether or not a Negro boy in a picture would like to be white, 74 per cent of a group of 95 children answered "he would."

Clark[75] participated in a symposium at Michigan State University in 1964. At that time he stated that the report given to the United States Supreme Court in 1954 included hundreds of studies that would indicate the following:

. . . as a minority group the children learned the inferior status to which they are assigned, as they observe the fact that they are almost always segregated and kept apart from others who are treated with more respect by the society as a whole, they often react with feelings of inferiority, and a sense of personal humiliation. Many become confused about

their own personal worth. On the one hand, like all
other human beings, they require a sense of dignity; on
the other hand, almost not anywhere in society, do they
find their own dignity as human beings respected by
others. Under these conditions the minority group
child is thrown into conflict with regard to his feelings about himself and his group. . . . This conflict
and confusion leads to self-hatred and rejection of his
own group.[76]

This statement accurately described the attitude of other reputed
authorities[77], [78] in regard to the Negro self-concept and its development in the past.

Research studies have shown a positive relationship between
self-concept and academic achievement in the Negro population.
Green and Farquhar[79] investigated a sample of eleventh-grade students in a northern urban educational system and found self-
concept to be the best predictor of academic success for Negro
students. An analysis of the data indicated correlations of .36
for Negro males and .64 for Negro females between self-concept and
academic achievement.

In a doctoral study Meyers[80] sought to ascertain the relationships between self-concept and school achievement and racial identity and school achievement for experimental and control groups of
23 good achieving and 23 poor achieving disadvantaged Negro boys.
She found support for the hypothesis that Negro boys from economi-
cally disadvantaged homes who had positive self-concepts would be
achievers (p = .01). Likewise, the hypothesis that Negro boys
were achievers would differ from those who were underachievers in
being more acceptable of their ethnic identity was supported (p =
.01).

Even though most arguments seemed to indicate a negative or
less than adequate concept of self for the Negro, Clark has fore-
seen a positive self-concept in the developmental stages. He
sensed a change as a result of the Brown versus Topeka decision
and the sit-ins, freedom rides and direct action which followed.
This change was forecase in the following manner:

        The ferment within the Negro communities through-
    out the nation . . . suggests to this observer . . .
    that the past cycle of negative reinforcements of per-
    sonal and community powerlessness is now being sup-
    planted by a more positive action. If this is true,
    it is now possible to postulate that this evidence of
    increasing community action and the mobilization of
    power within the ghetto is having (or will have) a
    positive effect on the self-image of Negro adults and
    young people.[81]

Johnson[82] has found evidence that would support Clark's be-
lief. In a controlled study he analyzed the racial attitudes of
(1) a group of Negro children and teenagers who were participating

in a Freedom School where they were being taught Negro history, and (2) a militant interracial civil rights group of teenagers. The results indicated that groups within the Negro community which emphasized a positive view of Negro history and those who actively support work to change the status of the Negro in America, have and hold positive attitudes toward Negroes.

Significant Others and Self-Concept

Recent longitudinal research concerning significant others has provided data relevant to this study. Brookover[83] and others developed the following propositions from general self-concept theory:

1. A functional limit on a student's ability to learn in school is set by his "self-concept of ability."
2. A student's self-concept of academic ability is acquired in interaction with his significant others through his perception of their "evaluations of his academic ability."
3. A student's self-concept of academic ability is an "intervening variable" between his perceptions of others and his attempts to learn in school.[84]

General research objectives and hypotheses were formulated from these propositions and the following findings were reported.

The evidence indicated that parents and other family members were more likely than any other category of persons to be significant others for adolescents during junior and senior high school years. Although the proportion of students naming friends as significant others was much lower than those naming parents, it increased during the six-year period. The influence of friends on self-concept of ability increased somewhat in later years. Less than half of the students identified teachers and other school personnel as significant others in the junior high school years, and this proportion declined during the later years.[85]

It was found that the evaluations which students perceived parents, friends and teachers held for them were consistently correlated with their self-concepts of ability. The correlations ranged from .50 to .77 over the six-year period. Changes in perceived evaluations were significantly related to changes in self-concept of ability over periods of one or two years.[86]

These findings in addition to the previously reported data which showed the relationship between the self-concept of ability and grade-point average (see page 23) caused the researchers to accept the theory that "perceived evaluations are a necessary and sufficient condition for self-concept of ability, but that self-concept of ability is only a necessary but not sufficient condition for achievement."[87] They also reasoned the hypothesis that self-concept of ability intervenes between the independent variable, perceived evaluations, and the dependent one, school achievement, was generally supported. Their acceptance of this hypothesis resulted from the findings that the correlations between perceived evaluations and grade-point averages were found to be less than the correlations between each of these variables and self-concept of ability.[88]

The relationship between the evaluations and expectations of significant others was an implied part of earlier treatment of social nature of self-concept. Sullivan[89] emphasized the role of significant others in the development of the self-structure. He was especially concerned with the role parents play in its early development. In infancy, he saw the family, in their efforts to meet the needs of the child, as the primary determinant of the self-structure. He felt that as the child matures, other persons with whom the child interacts become significant in meeting his needs and thereby contribute to a changing view of self. Parents, peers or friends and teachers were considered as those significant in the development of the self-structure.

Several investigators were concerned with the relationships between the evaluations and expectations of significant others, as filled by persons in one of the above capacities, and the self-evaluations of individuals.

In an investigation undertaken by Medinnus,[90] the relationship between parent-child relations and self-acceptance was considered. Forty-four members of an introductory psychology course were the subjects of this investigation. Among this group of 18-year olds, it was found that those high in self-acceptance and adjustment were likely to perceive their parents as loving but not neglectful or rejecting. Correlations between self-regard measures and evaluations of child-rearing practices were found to be higher for boys than girls.

Davids and Lawton[91] obtained measures of self-concept and mother-concept from a group of 11-year old normal boys and a group of 11-year old boys who were institutionalized for emotional disturbances. Indices of self-concepts and mother-concepts were derived from the direct and projective methods of assessment that were used. It was hypothesized that self-concepts and mother-concepts are positively associated. This prediction was confirmed in the normal group and generally supported by the findings from the emotionally disturbed group. As expected, the normal boys evidenced significantly higher self-concepts and mother-concepts.

A study relating children's perceptions of their teachers' feelings toward them to their self-perceptions, to achievement and to classroom behavior was conducted by Davidson and Lang.[92] A checklist of trait names was administered on two occasions to 203 children in grades four, five and six in a New York City public school. On the first administration the children were instructed to respond to the list in terms of their teachers' perceptions of them and on the second in terms of their perceptions of themselves. The children were rated by their teachers with respect to achievement and behavioral characteristics. It was found that children's perceptions of their teachers' feelings toward them correlated positively and significantly with self-perception (r = .82, p < .001). Further, it was found the more positive the children's perception of a teacher's feelings, the better was their academic achievement, and the more desirable their classroom behavior as rated by teachers.

Portugues and Feshback[93] designed a study to determine the effects of variations in teachers' reinforcement styles on imitative behavior in 96 children, ranging in age from 8 to 10 years and varying in personality and social background characteristics. The findings indicated more imitative behavior on the part of the advantaged members of the group, more imitative behavior on the part of girls in both groups and that positive teachers were imitated more frequently.

Manis[94] studied the relationship between peer interaction and self-concept by comparing the adjective checklist descriptions of a group of male college students with the estimates others made of them. This was accomplished by having the students describe each member, including themselves, in a group of eight students. Each student made sociometric choices, which were used to select a friend and a non-friend, among the members of his group. A sample of 36 friendship pairs and 28 pairs of non-friends were selected. After a six-week period of interaction, the students were retested. It was found that the students' self-concepts were significantly influenced by their friends' opinions of them, particularly when the friends were perceived in a favorable light. Yet it was found that the friends' perceptions of the students were not significantly influenced by the students' self-images. Increases in agreement of student-friend pairs were attributed to changes in the students' self-concept, rather than to changes in friends' perceptions of the students.

A part of the longitudinal study by Brookover and associates[95] involved an effort to enhance the self-concept of ability of low-achieving students at the ninth-grade level. A sample of 193 students was involved in the original experimental, placebo and control groups of this study. The strategy was to use three treatments designed to enhance the self-evaluations and expectations by: (1) increasing the expectations and evaluations parents held of their children's ability; (2) introducing an expert who communicated directly to students positive information about their academic ability; and (3) creating a new significant other in the form of a counselor whose high expectations and evaluations might be internalized by students. Pretest and posttest measures of self-concept of ability were administered. The experimental group involving parent treatment exhibited significant gains in self-concept of ability over the treatment period. No significant differences were found for the other experimental groups. A follow-up assessment of the treatment effects the year following treatment revealed no significant differences in self-concept of ability for any of the groups.[96]

In a study of 144 underachieving secondary school pupils de-

signed by Engle,[97] two experimental treatments focused on the role
of significant other. One experiment was designated the "warm
teacher" treatment and the other labeled the "peer leader" treatment. Both treatments were based on the need for a significant
other with whom an individual can identify and draw upon for emotional support, who is interested and friendly and who views one as
an individual worthy of dignity, respect and love. Control groups
were defined and achievement and self-concept instruments were administered. No significant differences in control and experimental groups were revealed for achievement or self-concept.

Helping Relationships

     People have been helping one another in one form or another
since the dawn of man. Many human relationships have served as
helping relationships. Snygg and Combs stated, "even the most
casual kinds of human contacts may serve to effect important
changes in our ways of perceiving."[98] In a more formal structure
they argued that psychological treatment has been carried on more
or less as part of the functions of teachers, parents and the
clergy for hundreds of years. Regardless of circumstances, they
recognized that even very ordinary situations involving two or
more people frequently evolve from each seeking to satisfy his own
need, that of the enhancement of self.

     Rogers has defined the helping relationship as "a relation-
ship in which at least one of the parties has the intent of pro-
moting the growth, development, maturity, improved functioning,
improved coping with life of the other."[99] The other, according
to Rogers, may be one individual or a group.

     For Snygg and Combs, the task of teaching was a helping rela-
tionship and "involved the creation of situations conducive to the
effective exploration and discovery of personal meaning."[100] For
them the efficient production of learning experiences for others
depended upon the skill of the teacher in using his personality
as an instrument for helping others learn. They saw no one way of
creating relationships with students. Effective teaching came
about as a result of teacher perceptions of the nature of people,
the goals and purposes of education, personal adequacy and effective methods of teaching. The atmosphere set for learning, they
felt, must be one that permits the student freedom from threat,
a feeling of acceptance and the development of a stable frame of
reference.

     These elements are common to the characteristics of a helping
relationship as evolved by Rogers.[101] Through a summarization of
the empirical research and his own clinical experiences he identified the following characteristics which he felt desirable for a
person undertaking a helping relationship. (1) He should be
trustworthy in his presentation of self; that is, he should be de-
pendably real and not attempt to cloak his feelings. (2) He
should be capable of accepting and expressing his feelings. (3)
He should permit himself to experience warmth, caring, liking and

respect in his attitudes for the person with whom he is involved. (4) He should hold his feelings separate from those of the person with whom he is involved. (5) He should permit the person with whom he is involved to develop a personality quite apart from his own; that is, the person with whom he is working should be free to model his own personality. (6) He should attempt to give empathic understanding. (7) He should receive the person with whom he is involved unconditionally. (8) He should be sensitive enough that his behavior will not pose an external threat. (9) He should free the person with whom he is involved from as much external evaluation as possible. (10) He should accept the whole potentiality of the person with whom he is involved, that is, not accept his potential as fixed.

All of these characteristics probably cannot be found in any one individual serving in the helping relationship. Yet, Rogers[102] contended that anyone working in the field of human relations should strive to perfect these characteristics.

Although there has been little research that is directly concerned with the helping relationship, several studies have been indicative of its possibilities. Research from family-child, counselor-client and teacher-pupil relationships have been informative.

At the Fels Institute, Baldwin, Kalhorn and Breese[103] made a study of parent-child relationships. Of the various clusters of parental attitudes toward children, the "acceptant-democratic" seemed to facilitate the greatest amount of growth. Children of such parents showed an increasing I.Q., more originality, greater emotional security and control, and less excitability than children from other types of homes. They were somewhat slow in their initial social ability, yet by the time they reached school age, they were popular, friendly, and nonaggressive leaders. Parents, whose attitudes were classified as "actively rejectant," produced children who showed slightly decreasing I.Q., poor use of the abilities they possessed and a lack of originality. Many of these children were emotionally unstable, rebellious, aggressive and quarrelsome.

Whitehorn and Betz[104] investigated the degree of success achieved by young resident physicians in working with schizophrenic patients on a psychiatric ward. They chose for study seven residents who had been outstanding by helping their patients and another seven whose patients had shown the least degree of improvement. The investigators examined all available evidence to discover how the two groups of residents differed. The successful physicians tended to work toward goals which were oriented to the personality of the patient, rather than seeing him as a case history or a descriptive diagnosis. Their work was based in active personal participation or a person-to-person relationship. The physicians developed relationships in which these patients placed trust and confidence in them.

A study conducted by Halkides[105] was based upon the hypothesis that there would be a significant relationship between the extent of constructive personality change in the client and four counselor variables. The variables were the degree of empathic understanding manifested by the counselor; the degree of unconditional positive regard manifested by the counselor; the extent to which the counselor was genuine; and the extent to which the counselor's response matched the client's expression in the intensity of affective expression. A group of 10 cases which could be classed as "most successful" were selected for study. Three judges listened to various recorded counselor-client interactions and rated them. The researcher found that a high degree of empathic understanding was associated with the more successful cases ($p = .001$). This was also found to be true for unconditional positive regard and counselor genuineness ($p = .001$).

Elements of the helping relationship were involved in a study by Flanders[106] in which he sought to determine the interplay between anxiety and achievement resulting from pupil-teacher interaction. Two experimentally produced climates, characterized as a "learner-centered" relationship and a "teacher-centered" relationship, were developed. In the learner-centered climate the teacher was acceptant and supportive of the student and problem-centered in his approach. In the teacher-centered climate the teacher was directive, demanding and sometimes deprecating in his behavior toward the individual. Anxiety was estimated by measures of pulse rate, galvanic skin responses and by the direction and intensity of students' positive and negative feelings. As a result of the data Flanders concluded that: (1) When a conflict arose, student behavior oriented to the handling of inter-personal anxiety took precedence over behavior oriented toward achievement. (2) Teacher-centered patterns of behavior led to hostility to the self or the teacher, aggressiveness, withdrawal and even emotional disintegration. (3) Learner-centered patterns of behavior elicited problems-orientation, decreased interpersonal anxiety and led to emotionally readjusting and integrative behavior.

Numerous studies have been undertaken in an effort to determine teacher characteristics conducive to an effective helping relationship with regard to school learning. Hamachek[107] recently completed a study of the research in this area. He found that teachers who are superior in encouraging motivation and learning in students seem to exhibit more of the following characteristics:

1. Willingness to be flexible, to be direct or indirect as the situation demands
2. Capacity to perceive the world from the students' point of view
3. Ability to personalize their teaching
4. Willingness to experiment, try out new things
5. Skill in asking questions (as opposed to seeing self as a kind of answering service)
6. Knowledge of subject matter and related areas
7. Skill in establishing definite examination procedures
8. Willingness to provide definite study helps
9. Capacity to reflect an appreciative attitude (evidenced

by nods, comments, smiles, etc.)
10. Conversational manner in teaching--informal, easy style[108]

Findings from Tutorial Programs

Little research has been undertaken in the area of tutorial programs. As late as 1967 James Noce commented in a publication prepared by the Tutorial Assistance Center, "Very little careful and responsible tutorial research and evaluation has been performed anywhere nationally to date."[109] Yet, a number of studies have been reported which have incorporated statistical designs that attempt to measure change in pupil self-concept, achievement and intelligence.

In Winnetka, Illinois, Freund[110] has reported the progress of the Project for Academic Motivation. This project was originally conceived as an inquiry into academic underachievement, especially among elementary school males. The project was financed by a Wieboldt Foundation grant and used knowledgeable volunteers in an effort to improve the underachievers' classroom performances and to provide them with much needed recognition.

The projects on which the volunteers and children worked were coordinated with the curriculum, and pupils shared their experiences with their classes. The instruction provided by the volunteers were not tutorial or remedial, but rather enriching in nature.

Controlled evaluation was a part of the design. Children were drawn from the third, fourth and fifth grades of the two participating schools. Premeasures and postmeasures were administered to the 64 underachieving children who had been randomly assigned to the experimental and control groups. Measures were taken for attendance; for growth in reading, arithmetic, language and spelling; for attitudinal development and for self-esteem. The analysis of these data showed that the experimental group improved significantly in attitudes toward reading, in confidence in applying such skills as use of the dictionary and reference books, in school attendance and in enjoyment of school life. The author concluded that while there was no evidence to indicate that the experimental group improved more than the control group in terms of academic achievement, it was possible that improved school attendance and improved attitudes toward school and school tasks might result in improved academic achievement.[111]

Baun[112] reported a tutorial project involving 85 college volunteers who tutored 250 Negro secondary school pupils in basic science, remedial reading and arithmetic in after-school situations. Tutoring was supplemented by cultural and informative field trips. School personnel gave basic methods of teaching to the volunteers prior to their undertaking the tutorial relationship. Evaluation of the program was primarily based on comments of the faculty, the tutored pupils and their parents. Teachers

33

stated that the major advantage of the tutorial program was an increased level of academic motivation which was leading to a higher quality of classroom work. Tutored pupils and their parents expressed positive comments about the program. In the spring, the American Reading Achievement Test was administered to the seventh-grade class which included 22 of the tutored pupils. The test results indicated a significant difference in reading achievement favoring the tutored group. They showed an average gain of nine months in comparison to a 4.6 months' gain for the untutored group over a period of six months.

A tutorial project reported by Gordon, Curran and Avila[113] was designed to improve pupils' attitudes toward school and to improve the self-concepts of pupils. As a part of their educational course work, college sophomores were assigned to tutor pupils who had or were having learning difficulties. The tutored sample consisted of 20 pupils each from two elementary schools and one junior high school. They were matched by age, sex and enrollment in the same classes with a control group in each of the schools. Tutor-pupil pairs worked in the tutorial relationship for one hour per week over a period of twenty weeks.

In an effort to measure behavior change, teachers were administered a pupil behavior instrument, the Behavior Description Chart, for each child. The instruments were completed by the teachers at the beginning and the end of the project. Gordon's How I See Myself self-concept instrument was administered in January and May. Tests failed to exhibit significant differences for the tutored group on the aspects of leadership, aggressiveness and withdrawal as measured by the Behavior Description Chart. Likewise, there were no significant differences between the pretest and posttest scores of the experimental group with relation to self-concept.[114]

Cloward[115] has reported an extensive evaluation program for the Mobilization for Youth tutorial program in New York City. In each of 11 centers, tenth- and eleventh-grade high school students tutored fourth- and fifth-grade pupils under the supervision of certified teachers. All of the tutees were reading below grade level according to tests administered by the schools. An experimental group of 410 pupils and a control group of 185 pupils were randomly selected. Among those assigned to tutoring sessions, some were tutored for four hours per week, some for only two hours. Each of the pupils was tutored in reading.

On comparing reading scores on pretests and posttests after a five-month period, it was found that tutees who received four hours of tutoring per week showed an increase in reading ability which was significantly greater than the control group. This did not hold true for the group which received only two hours of help per week. Further analysis of data indicated that the tutorial services did not produce a measurable change in school marks, school behavior ratings or pupil attitudes and aspirations.[116]

In Columbus, Ohio, the Teen Tutorial Program[117] was designed as a strategy for breaking the cycle of succeeding generations of children educationally deprived during their critical preschool years. The tutorial program involved 40 boys and girls in one junior high school in tutorial relationships with members of two kindergarten classes from a nearby school. One measure, I.Q., was reported for the kindergarteners during the period of the pilot study. The results from pretests and posttests indicated gains in I.Q. of 3.11 points for the experimental group and .47 point for the control group. A level of significance was not reported.

Experience and Intelligence

Through World War II, educators, psychologists and others working in the areas of intelligence and its measurement were primarily concerned with two schools of thought. According to Hunt,[118] who amassed a comprehensive review of the literature relating to intellectual development, the theoretical leaders of this period believed intelligence was fixed and immutable. In addition, they assumed that the individual's basic repertoire of intellectual responses and capacities were predetermined by heredity. These assumptions led to intelligence being defined as an inherited capacity which was viewed as a basic dimension of the individual person.

Due in large part to the efforts of research, authoritative opinion has been redirected since World War II. Developmental studies in child behavior and intelligence have been instrumental in gaining recognition for experience as a pertinent factor in intellectual development.

Dennis[119] investigated the behavioral development of 174 children, aged one to four years, in three Iranian orphanages. In two of the institutions infant development was greatly retarded, while in the third institution behavioral progress was much less retarded. The researcher believed the differences among the children resulted from a paucity of handling, including the failure to place children in the sitting and the prone positions, on the part of attendants in the institutions in which a greater amount of retardation was prevalent. The absence of experiences in these positions was believed to have retarded the children in regard to sitting alone and the onset of locomotion. Lack of experience in the prone position seemed to have prevented children from learning to creep; instead of creeping, the majority of children from the more retarded institutions, prior to walking, locomoted by scooting. In the other institution, where all children were frequently handled, propped in the sitting position and placed prone, motor development resembled that of home-reared children. Retardation was believed to have resulted from the lack of learning opportunities. Dennis concluded that the contribution of experience to the development of infant behavior must be acknowledged and that retardation cannot be explained by emotional, biological and maturational factors alone.

Working in a state orphanage, Skeels and Skodak[120] proposed to determine the effect of surroundings upon the measured intelligence of mentally retarded children. In the institution such children were placed in a sterile environment from infancy to age four. They were denied stimulating toys or things to look at as well as adult contacts. Adoption of these children was not permitted. For purposes of this study, it was proposed that an experimental group of 11 children be placed for care with women in wards for the mentally retarded. Twelve other children were assigned to a control group that remained in the orphanage and received the usual assigned treatment. The measured intelligence scores of the children assigned to the experimental group ranged from 36 to 89, while the scores of the control group ranged from 50 to 103. Over a two-year period each child in the experimental group showed a gain in I.Q. and the group's average was raised from 64 to 92. At the end of two years, the members of the experimental group were permitted to be adopted while the members of the control group remained in the institution. Following another two and one-half years, the average I.Q. of the experimental group was reported as 96 with no member having a score less than 90. Over the same period of time the members of the control group regressed from average I.Q. of 87 to an average of 66.

Several authorities have recognized the role experience plays in development of intelligence. Snygg and Combs, arguing from the perceptual point of view, stated, "intelligence is not something static and unchangeable. . . . It is a function of the richness, extent and availability of perceptions in the perceptual field and is open to change in the degree to which the phenomenal field itself can be changed."[121] Hunt, in drawing implications from his review of the literature, accepted that "the genes set the limits on the individual's potential for intellectual development." But he also argued, "they do not guarantee that this potential will be achieved and they do not, therefore, fix the level of intelligence as it is commonly measured." Hunt felt the evidence demanded new assessments of the development of intelligence concerned largely "with the experiential side of the matter where the genotype-environment interaction occurs."[122]

Disadvantaged groups have been the basis for many of Deutsch's studies. His research has been founded in part on the concept of "stimulus deprivation," which he has defined as "not a restriction of the quantity of stimulation, but, rather, a restriction to a segment of the spectrum of stimulation potentially available." He argued that a child from any circumstance who has been deprived of a substantial portion of the variety of stimuli which he is maturationally capable of responding to is likely to be deficient in the equipment required for learning. "This," he stated, "might be a crucial factor in the poorer performance of the lower socioeconomic children on standardized tests of intelligence."[123]

Deutsch and Brown[124] studied the intelligence test differences for a sample of 543 urban public school children, stratified by race, grade level (first and fifth grades) and social class. The intelligence test used was the Lorge-Thordike Test. A three-way analysis of variance was calculated using I.Q. scores as the dependent variable. The results indicated there were no significant differences in I.Q. scores with regard to grade level. Differences between scores of Negro and white children were highly significant (p <.001) and equally strong between socioeconomic levels. While the analysis of variance did not indicate a significant difference in race by socioeconomic interaction, an inspection of the means showed: (1) Negro children at each of the socioeconomic levels scored lower than the white children; and (2) that Negro-white differences increase at each higher socioeconomic level. While the children in each racial group showed gains in I.Q. with ascending socioeconomic level, gains for the white group appeared to be considerably greater.

Wilson[125] reported similar findings for a sample of students drawn from a population of elementary, junior and senior high school pupils in California. He found that the disparity in I.Q. scores between Negroes and whites increased over the school years. A difference of nine I.Q. points existed between the Negro and white test scores in the primary grades. The difference expanded to 15 points in senior high school. In addition, he found family socioeconomic status made a substantial difference in the performance of white pupils but made a negligible difference in Negro performance.

The views surrounding the development of programs designed to enhance intellectual development are conflicting. Deutsch[126] has developed programs at the preschool and primary levels specifically directed at such development. In a recent publication Deutsch advocated the use of intervention programs with this admonition:

> The task of a compensatory or an enrichment program . . . is to diagnose the deficits [of the child] and attempt to determine the kinds of procedures that ameliorate them. Part of both the diagnosis and the determination might involve an evaluation of what is missing from the child's background, followed by a study of how the missing might have contributed to his more advanced development. But there is no logic to an assumption that . . . a simple putting in of <u>now</u> of what was missing <u>then</u> will have a beneficial effect on the current <u>deficit</u> areas. This is not to say that some of the experiences missed should not be provided i.e., why not take the children to the zoo? But that experience should not be structured differently for the child: in terms of his current developmental level.[127]

In concluding his statements in <u>Intelligence and Experience</u>, Hunt[128] issued a strong statement that tends to support intervention. He felt it no longer unreasonable to consider that it might be feasible to govern the encounters that children have with their environments in order to achieve a substantially faster rate of intellectual development. He argued:

> The discovery of the ways to govern the encounters

children have with their environments for this purpose would require a great deal of expensive and difficult investigation of the effects of various kinds of early experience on later intellectual capacity. Even after the discovery of ways. . . . the tasks of effecting the necessary changes within the culture in child-rearing practices and in educational procedures would be Herculean.[129]

Nevertheless, Hunt mandated that if the present increasingly technological society was to continue to advance, then ways of increasing the intellectual capacity of the majority of the population must be undertaken.

A number of compensatory education programs were evaluated for the report, *Racial Isolation in the Public Schools*. The findings, which came from predominately Negro schools, indicated no significant gains in I.Q. or educational achievement as a result of the programs. The Civil Rights Commission, the group which prepared the report, extensively reviewed four of these programs and concluded that the evidence strongly suggested "compensatory education programs are not likely to succeed in racially and socially isolated school environments."[130]

A number of research reports have claimed I.Q. gains as a result of intervention programs. Deutsch[131] reported data from an enrichment program undertaken by the Institute for Developmental Studies. A group of four-year old children was selected to participate in a structured preschool program. A control sample, not initially different and coming from the same population, was also selected. When these groups entered first grade two years later, Deutsch defined another control group from the original population which had no preschool, kindergarten or testing experience. The mean Stanford-Binet Scale I.Q. for the six-year old control group was 85.5, whereas the mean I.Q.'s of the original groups were 98.9 and 99.

Weikart and Lambie[132] reported a preschool project that was conducted in the homes of 35 culturally disadvantaged families. Matched experimental and control groups were defined using the socioeconomic levels of the families and the children's I.Q.'s as criteria. For one and one-half hours per week a teacher visited the home of each participating family and worked with the mother and child on a carefully individualized educational program. The experimental group obtained a statistically significant greater change score on the Stanford-Binet Scale than did the control group.

A more subtle form of intervention was involved in research undertaken by Rosenthal and Jacobson.[133] The proposition that favorable expectations by teachers could lead to an increase in intellectual competence was tested in a public elementary school in a lower-class community of a medium-size city. All children in the school were pretested with the Flanagan Test of Mental Ability. The teachers in the school were informed that this test would predict intellectual "blooming" or "spurting." At the beginning of the following school year, each of the 18 teachers of grades one through six was given the names of the children in his classroom who would in the academic year ahead show dramatic intellectual growth. About 20 per cent of the school's children were alleged to be potential "spurters." The special children had actually been chosen by means of a table of random numbers.

All children in the school were retested with the same I.Q. test after one semester, after a full academic year and after two full academic years. For the first two retests the children were with the teacher who was given the "spurters" report; while for the final retesting all the children had been promoted to classes with teachers who did not possess knowledge of their special expectations. Gains in I.Q. from pretest to the various retests were computed for the members of the experimental and control groups. After the first year of the experiment, significant mean gains favoring the experimental group were found. During the follow-up year the younger children of the first two grades lost their gained advantage; while the children in upper grades exhibited even greater gains.[134]

Summary

Since the primary purpose of this study was to analyze the effects of enrichment tutoring upon the self-concept, the educational achievement and the measured intelligence of underachieving males in the inner-city elementary school, the review of the literature incorporated several relevant areas of concern. The salient findings of the review are related in the following paragraphs.

Social interaction has played a major role in most theoretical developments of self-concept. Most theorists seem to say that this factor is a major element in the evaluation of self. They are in general agreement that self-concept arises out of the individual's relationships with others.

Theorists have reasoned that self-concept is stable over periods of time. Yet, they have further agreed that under certain conditions, concepts of self may change. Although investigations have revealed a degree of stability over time, the indications are that self-concept can be changed. Some studies have shown that individuals possessing less than adequate pictures of self are more susceptible to changes in self-concept than those who possess an adequate self-picture.

Regardless of the fact that a majority of self-concept measurement has been performed with self-report devices, the literature offered numerous questions regarding the validity of these instruments. Some experts in the field argued that self-report instruments have been designed to measure well-defined constructs.

The implications from research seemed to establish a positive relationship between self-concept and educational achievement. Even though some researchers claimed an ordered relationship between the two variables, others argued that a direct causal relationship could not be established. Brookover's data appeared to indicate that self-concept of ability is a necessary but not sufficient condition for academic achievement.

Considering that there is little current empirical evidence to indicate a less than adequate Negro self-concept, many authorities have appeared to assume this is fact. In the past, evidence has suggested that this was true; yet today, some authorities might argue that this situation has been and is changing. The findings from research implied a positive relationship between self-concept and educational achievement for Negro students.

Brookover has found that parents, peers and school-related personnel are significant others for secondary school students. Data from his and other studies have indicated positive relationships between self-concept and the perceptions held by significant others. Two experiments contrived to interject significant others into the experiments of underachieving secondary students indicated few positive significant changes in self-concept.

In the literature characteristics of a positive helping relationship were detailed. Basically, the characteristics included: freedom from threat for the person being helped, empathic understanding on the part of the helper, and respect for the individual as well as his desires and potentials. Elements of positive helping relationships were incorporated into some research designs. In essence, these relationships were found to be "client-centered" or "learner-centered" in nature.

A number of tutorial programs have been studied. The findings from some of these programs implied significant positive changes for achievement and measured intelligence. Few programs were concerned with changes in self-concept as a result of tutoring. The results from one such program showed no significant differences in tutored and untutored pupils.

Recently those concerned with the study of intelligence have been more receptive to the role experience plays in intellectual development, especially as measured by standardized tests. Several experiments have shown relationships between experience and intellectual as well as motor development. Positive changes in measured intelligence have resulted from intervention programs. Intervention methods were designed to increase teacher expectations or to provide broader experiences. There was also evidence available to indicate some compensatory programs have resulted in little, if any, change in measured intelligence.

[1]William James, *Psychology* (New York: Henry Holt and Co., 1892), pp. 176-216.

[2]*Ibid.*, p. 177.

[3]*Ibid.*, p. 196.

[4]*Ibid.*, p. 179.

[5]Ruth Wylie, *The Self Concept* (Lincoln, Nebraska: University of Nebraska Press, 1961), p. 3.

[6]Mead, *op. cit.*, pp. 135-226.

[7]*Ibid.*, p. 171.

[8]Arthur T. Jersild, *Child Psychology* (Englewood Cliffs, New Jersey: Prentice Hall, Inc., 1960).

[9]*Ibid.*, p. 116.

[10]Snygg and Combs, *op. cit.*, pp. 126-127.

[11]*Ibid.*, p. 134.

[12]*Ibid.*, p. 127.

[13]Carl R. Rogers, *Client-Centered Therapy* (Boston: Houghton Mifflin Company, 1951).

[14]*Ibid.*, p. 498.

[15]*Ibid.*, p. 516.

[16]*Ibid.*, p. 517.

[17]David P. Ausubel, *Theory and Problems of Child Development* (New York: Grune and Stratton, 1958), p. 380.

[18]*Ibid.*, pp. 270-275.

[19]Victor C. Raimy, "Self-Reference in Counseling Intervention," *Journal of Counseling Psychology*, 12 (1948), pp. 153-156.

[20]Brookover and Gottlieb, *op. cit.*, pp. 468-469.

[21]*Ibid.*, p. 469.

[22]Brookover, Erickson and Joiner, *op. cit.*, p. 8.

[23]Prescott Lecky, *Self-Consistency: A Theory of Personality* (New York: Island Press, 1945).

[24]Snygg and Combs, *op. cit.*, p. 130.

[25]*Ibid.*, p. 163.

[26]Rogers (1951), *op. cit.*, pp. 505-515.

[27]Morris Rosenberg, *Society and the Adolescent Self-Image* (Princeton, New Jersey: Princeton University Press, 1965).

[28]*Ibid.*, pp. 150-152.

[29]Mary Engel, "The Stability of Self-Concept in Adolescence," *Journal of Abnormal and Social Psychology*, 58 (1959), pp. 211-215.

[30]*Ibid.*, p. 213.

[31]Warren A. Ketcham and William C. Morse, *Dimensions of Children's Social and Psychological Development Related to School Achievement* (Ann Arbor, Michigan: School of Education, University of Michigan, 1965).

[32]*Ibid.*, p. 204.

[33]Ira J. Gordon, *Studying the Child in School* (New York: John Wiley and Sons, Inc., 1966), pp. 52-88.

[34]Wylie, *loc. cit.*

[35]Gordon, *op. cit.*, p. 54.

[36]Wylie, *op. cit.*, pp. 6-8.

[37]Donald E. Super, "Theories and Assumptions Underlying Approaches to Personality Assessment," *Objective Approaches to Personality Assessment*, ed. Bernard M. Bass and Irvin A. Bay (Princeton, New Jersey: D. Van Nostrand Company, 1959), pp. 24-40.

[38]Wylie, *op. cit.*, pp. 40-110.

[39]William Stephenson, *The Study of Behavior: Q-Technique and Its Methodology* (Chicago: University of Chicago Press, 1953).

[40]Wylie, *loc. cit.*

[41]Rensis Likert, "A Technique for the Measurement of Attitudes," *Archives of Psychology*, 140 (1932), pp. 5-43.

[42]Wylie, *op. cit.*, pp. 23-24.

[43]*Ibid.*, p. 24.

[44]Combs, *loc. cit.*

[45]Rogers (1961), *op. cit.*, p. 207.

[46]Super, *op. cit.*, p. 35.

[47]John Dewey, *Democracy and Education* (New York: The MacMillan Co., 1916), pp. 334-335.

[48]Ernest R. Hilgard, "The Nature of Learning Theories," *Readings for Educational Psychology*, ed. William Fullagar *et al.* (New York: Thomas Y. Crowell Company, 1964).

[49]*Ibid.*, p. 4.

[50]Lee J. Cronbach, *Educational Psychology* (New York: Harcourt, Brace and Co., 1954), pp. 121-122.

[51]*Ibid.*, pp. 49-50.

[52]Robert M. W. Travers, *Essentials of Learning* (New York: The MacMillan Company, 1963), pp. 1-39.

[53]Henry Chauncey and John E. Dobbin, "Testing Has a History," *Readings in Educational and Psychological Measurement*, ed. Clinton I. Chase and H. Glenn Ludlow (Boston: Houghton-Mifflin Co., 1966), pp. 3-18.

[54]Howard W. Bernard, *Psychology of Learning and Teaching* (New York: McGraw-Hill Books, Inc., 1954).

[55]Wylie, *op. cit.*, pp. 199-202.

[56]Ira J. Gordon, "New Conceptions of Children's Learning and Development," *Learning and Mental Health in the School*, ed. Walter Waltzen (Washington, D. C.: Association for Supervision and Curriculum Development, N.E.A., 1966), pp. 49-73.

[57]Travers, *op. cit.*, p. 460.

[58]Jacob Schulman, "A Comparison Between Ninth and Twelfth Grade Students on Self-Estimates of Abilities and Objective Scores on the Differential Aptitude Test" (unpublished Ed.D. Dissertation, New York University, 1955).

[59]John McDavid, "Some Relationships Between Social Reinforcement and Scholastic Achievement," *Journal of Consulting Psychology*, 23 (1959), pp. 151-154.

[60]Ira J. Gordon, *Human Development: From Birth to Adolescence* (New York: Harper and Brothers, Inc., 1962), p. 380.

[61]Brookover, Erickson, and Joiner, *op. cit.*, pp. 142-143.

[62]Martin B. Fink, "Self-Concept as It Relates to Academic Underachievement," *California Journal of Educational Research*, 13 (1962), pp. 57-62.

[63]Melville C. Shaw, Kenneth Edson and Hugh Bell, "The Self-Concept of Bright Underachieving High School Students as Revealed by an Adjective Checklist," *Personnel and Guidance Journal*, 89 (1960), pp. 193-196.

[64]Stanley Coopersmith, "A Method for Determining Types of Self-Esteem," *Journal of Abnormal and Social Psychology*, 19 (1959), pp. 87-94.

[65]*Ibid.*, p. 90.

[66]Raymond F. Bodwin, "The Relationship Between Immature Self-Concept and Certain Educational Disabilities" (unpublished Ph.D. Dissertation, Michigan State University, 1957).

[67]Paul B. Campbell, "Self-Concept and Academic Achievement in Middle Grade Public School Children" (unpublished Ed.D. Dissertation, Wayne State University, 1965).

[68]Max Bruck, "A Study of Age Differences and Sex Differences in the Relationship Between Self-Concept and Grade-Point Average" (unpublished Ph.D. Dissertation, Michigan State University, 1957).

[69]Edward J. Hayes, "Relationships Between Self-Concept of Arithmetic and Arithmetic Achievement in a Selected Group of Sixth Grade Students" (unpublished Ph.D. Dissertation, College of Education, Michigan State University, 1967).

[70]Donald C. Butcher, "A Study of the Relationships of Student Self-Concept to Academic Achievement in Six High Achieving Elementary Schools" (unpublished Ed.D. Dissertation, Michigan State University, 1967).

[71]John C. Seymore, "The Relationship of Student Role Concept and Self-Concept of Academic Success and Satisfaction" (unpublished Ed.D. Dissertation, Columbia University, 1963).

[72]*Brown versus Board of Education of Topeka*, 347 U.S. 403 (1954).

[73]Kenneth B. Clark and Mamie P. Clark, "Racial Identification and Preference in Negro Children," *Reading in Social Psychology*, ed. T. M. Newcomb and E. L. Hartley (New York: Holt, 1947), pp. 169-178.

[74]Helen Trager and Miriam Yarrow, *They Learn What They Live* (New York: Harpers, 1952), pp. 141-142.

[75]Michigan State University, *Proceeding of a Symposium: A Symposium on School Integration* (East Lansing, Michigan: Bureau of Educational Research, Michigan State University, May, 1964).

[76]*Ibid.*, p. 4.

[77] David P. Ausubel and Pearl Ausubel, "Ego Development Among Segregated Negro Children," *Education in Depressed Areas*, ed. A. Harry Passow (New York: Teacher College, Columbia University, 1963), pp. 113-141.

[78] Jean D. Grambs, "The Self-Concept: Basis for Reeducation of Negro Youth," *The Negro Self-Concept*, ed. William C. Kvaraceus (New York: McGraw-Hill, 1965), pp. 1-10.

[79] Robert L. Green and William Farquhar, "Negro Academic Motivation and Scholastic Achievement," *Journal of Educational Psychology*, 56 (1965), pp. 241-243.

[80] Edna O. Myers, "Self-Concept, Family Structure and School Achievement: A Study of Disadvantaged Negro Boys" (unpublished Ed.D. Dissertation, Columbia University, 1966).

[81] Michigan State University, *op. cit.*, p. 12.

[82] David W. Johnson, "Racial Attitudes of Negro Freedom School Participants and Negro and White Civil Rights Participants," *Social Forces*, 45 (1966), pp. 266-273.

[83] Brookover, Erickson and Joiner, *op. cit.*

[84] *Ibid.*, p. 44.

[85] *Ibid.*, pp. 140-141.

[86] *Ibid.*, pp. 141-142.

[87] *Ibid.*, pp. 142-143.

[88] *Ibid.*, pp. 142-144.

[89] Harry S. Sullivan, *The Interpersonal Theory of Psychiatry* (New York: W. W. Norton and Company, Inc., 1953).

[90] Gene R. Medinnus, "Adolescents' Self Acceptance and Perception of Their Parents," *Journal of Consulting Psychology*, 29 (1965), pp. 150-154.

[91] Anthony Davids and Marcia J. Lawton, "Self-Concept, Mother-Concept and Food Aversion in Emotionally Disturbed and Normal Children," *Journal of Abnormal and Social Psychology*, 62 (1961), pp. 309-314.

[92] Helen H. Davidson and Gerhard Lang, "Children's Perceptions of Their Teachers' Feelings Toward Them Related to Self Perception, School Achievement and Behavior," *Journal of Experimental Education*, 29 (1960), pp. 107-118.

[93] Stephen H. Portuges and Norma D. Feshback, "The Effects of Teachers' Reinforcement Style Upon Imitative Behavior of Children,"

A.E.R.A. Paper Abstracts, ed. Henry Hausdorf (Washington, D. C.: American Educational Research Association, 1968), p. 268.

[94] Melvin Manis, "Social Interaction and the Self-Concept," *Journal of Abnormal and Social Psychology*, 51 (1955), pp. 362-370.

[95] Brookover, Lapere, *et al., op. cit.*

[96] Brookover, Erickson and Joiner, *op. cit.*

[97] Kenneth B. Engle, "An Exploratory Study of Significant Others in Producing Change in Self-Concept and Achievement in Secondary School Underachievers" (unpublished Ed.D. Dissertation, Michigan State University, 1964).

[98] Snygg and Combs, *op. cit.*, pp. 410-420.

[99] Rogers (1961), *op. cit.*, pp. 39-57.

[100] Snygg and Combs, *op. cit.*, pp. 383-409.

[101] Rogers (1961), *loc. cit.*

[102] *Ibid.*

[103] Alfred L. Baldwin, Joan Kalhorn, and Fay H. Breese, "Patterns of Parent Behavior," *Psychological Monographs*, 58 (1945), pp. 1-75.

[104] John C. Whitehorn and Barbara J. Betz, "A Study of Psychotherapeutic Relationships Between Physicians and Schizophrenic Patients," *American Journal of Psychiatry*, 111 (1954), pp. 321-331.

[105] Galatia Halkides, "An Investigation of Therapeutic Success as a Function of Therapist Variables" (unpublished Ph.D. Dissertation, University of Chicago, 1958).

[106] Ned A. Flanders, "Personal-Social Anxiety as a Factor in Experimental Learning Situations," *Journal of Educational Research*, 45 (1951), pp. 100-110.

[107] Don E. Hamachek, "Motivation in Learning," a pamphlet in the *What Research Says to the Teacher Series* (Washington, D. C.: Association of Classroom Teachers of the National Education Association, 1968), pp. 1-15.

[108] *Ibid.*, p. 15.

[109] James Noce, *Research and Evaluation in Tutorial Programs* (Washington, D. C.: Tutorial Assistance Center, 2115 S. Street, N. W., 1967), p. 1.

[110] Janet Freund, "Time and Knowledge to Share," *Elementary School Journal*, 65 (1965), pp. 351-358.

[111]*Ibid.*

[112]Eugene Baun, "The Washington University Campus Y Tutoring Project," *Peabody Journal of Education*, 43 (1965), pp. 161-168.

[113]Ira J. Gordon, Robert L. Curran and Donald L. Avila, *An Inter-Disciplinary Approach to Improving the Development of Culturally Disadvantaged Children* (Gainesville, Florida: College of Education, University of Florida, 1966).

[114]*Ibid.*, pp. 15-25.

[115]Robert D. Cloward, "The Nonprofessional in Education: Mobilization for Youth's Tutorial Project," *Educational Leadership*, 24 (1967), pp. 604-606.

[116]*Ibid.*

[117]Gene Telego, "A Teen Tutorial Program," *Pacereport* (Lexington, Kentucky: A publication of the College of Education, University of Kentucky, May-June, 1968), pp. 15-17.

[118]Joseph McV. Hunt, *Intelligence and Experience* (New York: The Ronald Press Co., 1961), p. 347.

[119]Wayne Dennis, "Causes of Retardation Among Institutionalized Children: Iran," *Journal of Genetic Psychology*, 96 (1960), pp. 47-59.

[120]Bernard Asbell, "The Case of the Wandering I.Q.'s," *Redbook*, 129 (1967), pp. 31-36.

[121]Snygg and Combs, *op. cit.*, pp. 222-223.

[122]Hunt, *op. cit.*, p. 7.

[123]Martin Deutsch, "The Disadvantaged Child and the Learning Process," *The Disadvantaged Child*, ed. Martin Deutsch (New York: Basic Books, Inc., 1967), pp. 44-46.

[124]Martin Deutsch and Bert R. Brown, "Social Influences in Negro-White Intelligence Differences," *The Disadvantaged Child*, ed. Martin Deutsch (New York: Basic Books, Inc., 1967), pp. 295-307.

[125]Alan B. Wilson, "Educational Consequences of Segregation in a California Community," *Racial Isolation in the Public Schools*, *Vol. II* by U. S. Civil Rights Commission (Washington, D. C.: U. S. Government Printing Office, 1967), pp. 171-174.

[126]Martin Deutsch, "Social Intervention and the Malleability of the Child," *The Disadvantaged Child*, ed. Martin Deutsch (New York: Basic Books, Inc., 1967), pp. 1-29.

[127]*Ibid.*, p. 11.

[128]Hunt, *op. cit.*, p. 363.

[129]*Ibid.*

[130]U. S. Civil Rights Commission, *Racial Isolation in the Public Schools, Vol. I* (Washington, D. C.: U. S. Government Printing Office, 1967), pp. 115-140.

[131]Deutsch, *loc. cit.*

[132]David P. Weikart and Delores Z. Lambie, "Preschool Intervention Through a Home Teaching Project," *A.E.R.A. Paper Abstracts* (Washington, D. C.: American Educational Research Association, 1968), pp. 86-87.

[133]Robert Rosenthal and Lenore Jacobson, *Pygmalion in the Classroom* (New York: Holt, Rinehart and Winston, Inc., 1968).

[134]*Ibid.*, pp. 175-176.

CHAPTER 3

DESIGN AND METHODOLOGY

This research was designed to study the effectiveness of enrichment tutoring. The design and methods used in the study are described under the following headings: (1) Design; (2) Setting; (3) Recruitment of Volunteers to Perform as Enrichment Tutors; (4) Sample; (5) Treatment; (6) Instrumentation and Collection of Data; (7) Statistical Hypotheses; and, (8) Procedures for Analyzing the Data.

Design

In this study the experimental method was employed. Good, Barr and Scates considered this technique to be among the major types of educational research. For them, ". . . the experimental technique, whether used in the classroom or laboratory, has possibilities for the solution of numerous and significant problems through the process of controlled evaluation and measurement."[1] The primary problem they saw confronting the researcher who employed the experimental method resulted from the lack of control with respect to the variables associated with human behavior.

One experimental method recognized by Good and associates[2] was the parallel-group technique. This procedure involved the use of two or more equivalent groups at the same time. When utilizing this method, a single variable under carefully controlled conditions was manipulated. The variable represented the experimental factor applied to one or more of the groups. The remaining group, which followed a customary or non-experimental procedure, served as control for comparative purposes. The most difficult aspect of this procedure, they felt, was the equating of experimental and control groups.

The design selected for this study was the pretest-posttest control group design, a form of the parallel-group technique, delineated by Campbell and Stanley.[3] In this design random assignment was made to experimental and control groups. After assignments were made, observations of a measured form were taken of the two groups. Once the observations were taken, the experimental group received the treatment and the control group continued in the usual fashion. Observations of the group were also taken at the close of the experiment, and comparisons between mean gains of the groups were made.

The major problem with this design, as seen by Good and associates, revolved about the equating of experimental and control groups. For Campbell and Stanley[4] the equation of groups was accomplished through random assignment to control and experimental groups. Rummel also accepted randomization as a method used to establish equivalent groups.[5]

In addition to the testing program, an open-ended questionnaire was administered to the participating teachers at the close of the program. The questionnaire was designed as an instrument to determine the effectiveness of the enrichment tutorial program from the classroom teacher's point of view.[6]

Setting

The school selected to participate in this study was located in a Midwestern industrial city with a population of approximately 200,000. It was one of a group of 14 elementary schools selected by the local Board of Education for inclusion in compensatory education programs developed for inner-city schools. These schools shared, at least in part, the problems of low educational achievement, racial imbalance, a population of predominately lower-income families and the limitations of space generally found in schools located in the city core.

The city's Negro population represented about 23% of its total population. In the public schools, the Negro population accounted for approximately 35% of the total. In the 14 schools included among the inner-city group, the proportion of Negro population generally was higher than the average Negro population in the schools. During the 1967-68 school year the Negro population in the participating school accounted for more than 95% of the total school population.

Because of the location of a new school in the vicinity and the accompanying changes in school attendance areas, the number of students in the participating school was less than that of the preceding year. A primary reason for locating the program in this school resulted from the space made available by the smaller school population. Several spaces were available to serve as a workspace for the enrichment tutors. The decision was made to place the enrichment tutors in a workspace apart from the regular school program. In this manner the regular school routine was less likely to be disrupted. A temporary classroom unit located on the school grounds was assigned as the workspace.

In an effort to provide a degree of privacy in the tutorial sessions, the unit was divided into six individual work areas. The separation of the work areas was accomplished by the use of inexpensive partitions. Classroom furniture and instructional supplies and materials were placed in each of the work areas.

In order to provide ready assistance to enrichment tutors, when problems arose, the supervisors of the program were provided a work area in the workspace. In addition, storage space for enrichment and instructional supplies and materials was located in the unit.

Recruitment of Volunteers to
Perform as Enrichment Tutors

After consultation with the representatives of the school
district in which the program of enrichment tutoring was undertaken, the recruitment of volunteer enrichment tutors was initiated. The leaders of community organizations were approached regarding the possible participation of their memberships in the
program. Organizations contacted for this purpose included: a
local volunteer bureau, student volunteer organizations from institutions of higher learning, retired teachers' organizations,
senior citizens' groups, the local Big Brothers' organization and
several civic groups. Possible volunteers were referred to the
supervisors of the enrichment tutorial program for individual in-
terviews.

An assessment of existing tutorial programs led the supervisors of the program to screen the volunteers with regard to the
following guidelines:

1. The enrichment tutor will be a person who has met with
    success in his educational experiences.

2. The enrichment tutor will possess a desire to work with
    an underachieving pupil in a free and open capacity,
    i.e., the relationship will be pupil-oriented.

3. The enrichment tutor will exhibit an emotional balance
    acceptable to the supervisors of the program.

During the interview, full details of the program were related to
the potential enrichment tutor. If the volunteer met the require-
ments of the program, he was informed of his tentative acceptance,
pending the approval of school representatives.

In this manner, a total of 32 volunteer enrichment tutors
were recruited for the program. Of the 32 volunteers, 28 were recruited from student groups from institutions of higher learning,
two through senior citizens' organizations, one from a retired
teachers' group and one through the volunteer bureau.

Sample

An underachiever, as defined for the purpose of this study,
was a male pupil enrolled in a second-, third- or fourth-grade
class and who, in addition to being defined as an underachiever by
his classroom teacher, scored two months or more below grade level
on the California Achievement Test, 1963 Revision. Pupils designated as mentally retarded or emotionally disturbed by the criteria of the school system were excluded from tutorial participation.

Thirteen classroom teachers were assigned to classes at the
second-, third- and fourth-grade levels within the participating

school. All members of this group volunteered to have pupils in their classes involved in the experiment. From their classes a total of 72 pupils were identified as possible underachievers.

In late October achievement tests were administered to the 72 pupils identified by the classroom teachers. The results from the achievement tests indicated that five members of the group were achieving at levels above the designated cutoff point for participation in the program. Two additional pupils moved from the school's attendance area before the program was initiated.

As a result of the achievement test data and pupils' movement from the school's attendance area, two teachers who no longer had pupils eligible for participation were eliminated from those who volunteered to become involved in the enrichment tutorial program. Sixty-five pupils drawn from the classrooms of the 11 remaining teachers met the criteria for participation in the program.

Since 32 enrichment tutors were recruited for service in the program, 32 of the 65 eligible pupils were assigned to experimental groups, and 33 pupils were assigned to the control groups. The pupils were stratified by grade level and then randomly assigned on a proportional basis by grade level to experimental and control groups. Random assignments were accomplished through the use of a table of random numbers and the randomization procedures delineated by Freund.[7] The original assignments to experimental and control groups are included in Table 3.1.

TABLE 3.1.--Original assignments to control and experimental groups by grade level.

	Experimental Group	Control Group	Total by Grade Level
Grade Level 2	12	12	24
Grade Level 3	9	9	18
Grade Level 4	11	12	23
Total	32	33	65

Over the period of treatment five members of the original group were, due to either movement from the school district or placement in special educational situations, dropped from the experimental or control groups.

Movement from the school district resulted in the loss of two members of the total group. One pupil lost in this manner was a member of the second-grade control group and the other was a member of the second-grade experimental group.

Two pupils became eligible for placement in special education classes for the mentally retarded. One of these two was a member of the third-grade control group, while the other was assigned to the experimental group at the fourth-grade level.

The final member not included in the total sample was a fourth-grade level member of the control group who was advanced to the fifth-grade level during the period of treatment. It seemed possible that his movement to the next higher grade level might influence the data, and he was therefore excluded from the final analysis of data.

The final analysis of the data included a total of 60 pupils in the three experimental and three control groups. A summary of the assignments to experimental and control groups for the analysis is presented in Table 3.2.

TABLE 3.2.--Summary by grade levels of pupils included in analysis.

	Experimental Group	Control Group	Total by Grade Level
Grade Level 2	11	11	22
Grade Level 3	9	8	17
Grade Level 4	10	11	21
Total	30	30	60

Since pupils were randomly assigned to experimental and control groups, the assumption was made that the groups at the various grade levels were equivalent with respect to the pretest self-concept scores, educational achievement level scores and measured intelligence scores. Due to the small size of the groups included in this study, questions with regard to their equivalency were posed.[8] The method utilized to analyze the data, the analysis of covariance, in effect, equated the experimental and control groups; and therefore concern for this assumption was eliminated.[9]

Treatment

The findings from the review of the literature seemed to indicate that the characteristics of a positive helping relationship represented an acceptable avenue of approach to enrichment tutoring. These characteristics have appeared to increase the probability of success in several experimental programs. By utilizing an approach evolved from these characteristics, it seemed likely that the enrichment tutors could perhaps become significant

others for the underachievers with whom they were assigned to
work.

Prior to his assignment to an enrichment tutor, each pupil
who was selected for participation in the program was approached
to determine his willingness to become involved. Each of the selected pupils expressed a desire to participate in the program.
After determining the pupil's interest, his parents were contacted
with regard to the program. An explanation of the program and its
aims was presented to them. Without exception, parental permis-
sion was granted for each member of the selected group to participate.

Upon pupil and parental clearance, the pairings of enrichment tutors and pupils were undertaken. An individual program
was developed for each of the pairs. The program was constructed
about the needs of the child as delineated by the classroom teacher and other members of the school staff. Needs were delineated
in social, psychological and academic areas. Program development
involved the cooperative efforts of the enrichment tutor, the
classroom teacher, other members of the school staff, parents and
the supervisors of the enrichment tutorial program. Each program
incorporated enrichment as well as tutorial tasks.

The enrichment tutors approached the tutorial and enrichment
tasks with their assigned pupils in a non-rigid, empathic and understanding manner. In addition, they expected and encouraged the
youngsters to perform in accord with their potential.

The enrichment tutor-pupil pairs devoted a minimum of one
hour per week to the tasks of the program during school hours.
This time was spent in the workspace or on field trips into the
community. In addition to the in-school contacts, the enrichment
tutors had social contacts with their assigned youngsters outside
the confines of the school day. Each enrichment tutor was asked
to commit himself to the tutorial relationship for the duration of
the school year.

Several efforts were directed toward maintaining program con-
tinuity. Before the program was initiated, an orientation session
was held. After the program was under way, the supervisors provided consultation time at the convenience of the enrichment tutor. The program director published a monthly newsletter and held
breakfast meetings with the enrichment tutors every other week.

Instrumentation and
Collection of Data

Four instruments were used to collect the data for this
study. Three of the instruments measured change in pupils as a
result of enrichment tutoring, while the fourth requested teachers' opinions regarding the effectiveness of enrichment tutoring.

Before and after treatment measures of self-concept, educational achievement and measured intelligence were administered to the experimental and control groups.

   Measure of self-concept.--The method used to study pupil self-concept was the Coopersmith Self-Esteem Inventory (CSEI). The raw scores were used to report pupil self-concept. The inventory as presented by Ketcham and Morse[10] included three subscales within its 42 items. The subscales were: (1) a self-measure that relates how the individual perceives himself (26 items); (2) a social self-measure that relates how the individual perceives himself socially (8 items); and (3) a school self-measure that relates how the individual perceives his school life (8 items).

   When a pupil is administered the instrument, he is asked to respond to each of the 42 items. The following items are similar in nature to those to which the pupil responds:

	LIKE ME	UNLIKE ME
I'm a hard worker.	X	
I am often unhappy.		X

If the statement is a description of how the pupil usually feels, he is told to place a check mark in the "LIKE ME" column. If the statement does not reflect how the pupil usually feels, he is instructed to place a check mark in the "UNLIKE ME" column. In addition, he is informed there are no right or wrong answers to the statements.[11]

   The instrument is scored on the basis of the pupil's responses which indicate high self-esteem. When Coopersmith developed the instrument, it was submitted to a group of five psychologists who sorted the items into two groups, those which indicated high self-esteem and those which indicated low self-esteem.[12] Raw scores for the three subscales are calculated by summing the "LIKE ME" and "UNLIKE ME" items which the pupil answered in the direction of high self-esteem. A raw score range of 0 to 26 is possible on the self-subscale while raw score ranges of 0 to 8 are obtainable on the subscales for social self and school self. The total raw score for the instrument is computed by adding the raw scores for the three subscales.[13]

   Coopersmith[14] administered the instrument to fifty- and sixth-grade classes of boys and girls. After a five-week interval, he calculated a test-retest reliability of .88. No significant differences were obtained for boys and girls.

   Dyer[15] designed a study to assess the confidence one might place in Coopersmith's instrument. Ten sample groups, each consisting of approximately 50 boys and girls from the third-, fifth-, seventh-, ninth- and eleventh-grade levels, were administered the instrument. He found reliability coefficients ranging from .63 to

.68 for males and .52 through .72 for females. For the total sample he reported a reliability coefficient of .65. Dyer felt the reliabilities to be excellent for the total self, self-subscale and the social self-subscale.

Because of the age and achievement levels of the pupils included in this study, this instrument was read to the pupils. For the same reasons the instruments were administered individually.

Measures of Educational Achievement.--The California Achievement Test, Form W, Lower Primary, 1957 Edition, and the California Achievement Test, Form W, Upper Primary, 1957 Edition (CAT), were the instruments used to measure educational achievement. Grade level equivalent scores which were derived from the tests' raw scores were used to report educational achievement.

The Lower Primary and Upper Primary batteries of this test are composed of achievement subtests in reading, arithmetic and language. The reading achievement subtests are divided into reading vocabulary and reading comprehension areas with raw scores reported for both. Raw scores are also calculated for the arithmetic reasoning and fundamental areas of the arithmetic subtests. The language achievement subtests are composed of two parts relating to the mechanics of English and spelling with a raw score reported for each area. Raw scores are computed for the various achievement subtests by combining the raw scores of their parts. A total achievement raw score is calculated by combining the raw scores of the subtests.

The manuals[16, 17] which accompanied the tests were used to convert the raw scores of total achievement, total reading achievement, total arithmetic achievement and total language achievement into grade level equivalents. In the manuals reliability coefficients of .95 and .98 were reported for total achievement on the Lower Primary and Upper Primary batteries, respectively. Reliability coefficients for the various achievement subtests and their subdivisions, the method used to compute the reliability coefficients and the norms for the tests are also reported in the manuals.

Measures of Intelligence.--The data for measured intelligence were collected through the use of Level 1 and Level 1H of the California Short-Form Test of Mental Maturity, 1963-S Form (CTMM). Language I.Q., non-language I.Q. and total I.Q. scores as derived from the raw scores of the batteries were used to report measured intelligence.

Raw scores are obtained from the following areas measured by both levels of the test: opposites, similarities, analogies, numerical values, number problems, verbal comprehension and delayed recall. A raw score for the non-language factor of the test is derived by combining the raw scores for opposites, similarities, analogies and numerical values. By combining the raw scores for number problems, verbal comprehension and delayed recall, a raw score for the language factor of the test is computed.

The combination of the raw scores for the language and non-language factors of the test give a total raw score for the test.

The manuals[18, 19] that accompanied the tests contained tables for converting the raw scores to I.Q. scores. Reliability data based on 1965 norms were reported in the manual[20] which accompanied Level 1H of the test. The reliability coefficient reported for total I.Q. was .92 and replaced the reliability data reported in the Technical Report on the California Test of Mental Maturity Series, 1963 Revision.[21] The reliability coefficient for total I.Q. on Level 1 of the test was reported as .94 in the latter manual. The reliability data for the language and non-language factors, the method of computing reliability and the normative data are also reported in the manuals cited above.

The three instruments used at the various grade levels to measure change in pupils and the times of pretest and posttest administrations are summarized in Table 3.3.

TABLE 3.3.--Summary of instrumentation by grade levels and the dates of pretest and posttest administration.

	Grade Levels	Date of Pretest	Date of Posttest
CSEI	2, 3, 4	Nov., 1967	May, 1968
CAT:			
Lower Primary Level	2	Oct., 1967	April, 1968
Upper Primary Level	3, 4	Oct., 1967	April, 1968
CTMM:			
Level 1	2, 3	Nov., 1967	May, 1968
Level 1H	4	Nov., 1967	May, 1968

Teachers' Opinions.--At the close of the school year, 10 of the 11 teachers whose pupils had received enrichment tutoring completed questionnaires designed to seek their opinions regarding the program. The questionnaire, the Teacher Evaluation Form, was a revision of an instrument used to evaluate another tutorial program.[22]

Two items on the questionnaire related to changes in pupils. They were question number one, which requested the most noteworthy aspects of enrichment tutoring, and question number four, which requested information about how the teacher felt enrichment tutoring assisted the participating pupils.

Statistical Hypotheses

The primary and subsidiary research hypotheses were broadly stated in Chapter I. The statistical hypotheses were formulated in a more specific form. For each dependent variable, i.e., self-concept, educational achievement and measured intelligence, a composite or total score was available. A major statistical hypothesis was developed for each of these variables. In addition, subhypotheses were cast for each of the components of the dependent variables.

The major statistical hypotheses were denoted by one-digit numbers following the word "hypothesis." Two-digit numbers following the word "hypothesis" indicated a subhypothesis. The first digit denoted the major variable, and the second digit related the component of the dependent variable under consideration. Ho was used to indicate a null hypothesis, while Ha was used to indicate an alternate hypothesis.

The following legend holds for each of the hypotheses: M_1 = tutored group; M_2 = non-tutored group.

Primary Research Hypothesis (Self-Concept) Converted to Statistical Hypotheses.--A major statistical hypothesis was developed for the composite self-concept (1). Statistical subhypotheses were developed for each of its components: the self-concept subscale (11), the social self-concept subscale (12), and the school self-concept subscale (13). Each hypothesis was tested at the second-, third- and fourth-grade levels.

Null Hypothesis 1: No difference will be found between tutored and non-tutored groups for composite self-concept as measured by average CSEI performance.

$$Ho_1: \quad M_1 = M_2$$

Alternate Hypothesis 1: The tutored group mean score for the composite self-concept of the CSEI will exceed that of the non-tutored group.

$$Ha_1: \quad M_1 > M_2$$

Null Hypothesis 11: No difference will be found between tutored and non-tutored groups on the self-concept subscale as measured by average CSEI performance.

$$Ho_{11}: \quad M_1 = M_2$$

Alternate Hypothesis 11: The tutored group mean score on the self-concept subscale of the CSEI will exceed that of the non-tutored group.

$$Ha_{11}: \quad M_1 > M_2$$

Null Hypothesis 12: No difference will be found between
tutored and non-tutored groups on the social self-
concept subscale as measured by average CSEI performance.

$$Ho_{12}: \quad M_1 = M_2$$

Alternate Hypothesis 12: The tutored group mean score on
the social self-concept subscale of the CSEI will exceed that of the non-tutored group.

$$Ha_{12}: \quad M_1 > M_2$$

Null Hypothesis 13: No difference will be found between
tutored and non-tutored groups on the school self-
concept subscale as measured by average CSEI performance.

$$Ho_{13}: \quad M_1 = M_2$$

Alternate Hypothesis 13: The tutored group mean score
on the school self-concept subscale of the CSEI will
exceed that of the non-tutored group.

$$Ha_{13}: \quad M_1 > M_2$$

Subsidiary Research Hypothesis (Educational Achievement) Converted to Statistical Hypotheses.--A major statistical hypothesis
was developed for total educational achievement (2). Statistical
subhypotheses were developed for each of its components: reading
achievement (21), arithmetic achievement (22), and language
achievement (23). Each hypothesis was tested at the second-,
third- and fourth-grade levels.

Null Hypothesis 2: No difference will be found between
tutored and non-tutored groups for total educational
achievement as measured by average CAT performance.

$$Ho_2: \quad M_1 = M_2$$

Alternate Hypothesis 2: The tutored group mean score for
total educational achievement on the CAT will exceed
that of the non-tutored group.

$$Ha_2: \quad M_1 > M_2$$

Null Hypothesis 21: No difference will be found between tutored and non-tutored groups for reading achievement as measured by average CAT performance.

$$Ho_{21}: \quad M_1 = M_2$$

Alternate Hypothesis 21: The tutored group mean score for reading achievement on the CAT will exceed that of the non-tutored group.

$$Ha_{21}: \quad M_1 > M_2$$

Null Hypothesis 22: No difference will be found between tutored and non-tutored groups for arithmetic achievement as measured by average CAT performance.

$$Ho_{22}: \quad M_1 = M_2$$

Alternate Hypothesis 22: The tutored group mean score for arithmetic achievement on the CAT will exceed that of the non-tutored group.

$$Ha_{22}: \quad M_1 > M_2$$

Subsidiary Research Hypothesis (Measured Intelligence) Converted to Statistical Hypotheses.--A major statistical hypothesis was developed for total measured intelligence (3). Statistical subhypotheses were developed for each of its components: language measured intelligence (31) and non-language measured intelligence (32). Each hypothesis was tested at the second-, third- and fourth-grade levels.

Null Hypothesis 3: No difference will be found between tutored and non-tutored groups for total measured intelligence as measured by average CTMM performance.

$$Ho_3: \quad M_1 = M_2$$

Alternate Hypothesis 3: The tutored group mean score for total measured intelligence on the CTMM will exceed that of the non-tutored group.

$$Ha_3: \quad M_1 > M_2$$

Null Hypothesis 31: No difference will be found between tutored and non-tutored groups for language measured intelligence as measured by average CTMM performance.

$$Ho_{31}: \quad M_1 = M_2$$

Alternate Hypothesis 31: The tutored group mean score for language measured intelligence on the CTMM will exceed that of the non-tutored group.

$$Ha_{31}: \quad M_1 > M_2$$

Null Hypothesis 32: No difference will be found between tutored and non-tutored groups for non-language measured intelligence as measured by average CTMM performance.

$$Ho_{32}: \quad M_1 = M_2$$

Alternate Hypothesis 32: The tutored group mean score for non-language measured intelligence on the CTMM will exceed that of the non-tutored group.

$$Ha_{32}: \quad M_1 > M_2$$

Procedures for Analyzing the Data

The analysis of the data incorporated two phases. The first phase involved the statistical analysis of the data derived from the measures of self-concept, educational achievement and intelligence that were taken. The second phase included the analysis of teachers' responses to items related to pupil change on the Teacher Evaluation Form.

Statistical Analysis.--The analysis of covariance was used to test each of the null hypotheses of this study. This technique was selected as the method of analysis because it increased the precision of the pretest-posttest control group design.[23, 24]

Popham[25] reported that this method of analysis is an extension of the analysis of variance coupled with features of regression analysis. He felt that through this technique the researcher is enabled to statistically equate the independent variable of the groups with respect to one or more control variables which are relevant to the dependent variable. Essentially, he argued that this method permitted the study of the performances of several groups which are unequal with regard to an important variable as though they are equal. For the purposes of this study, the respective pretests were used as control variables.

In essence the analysis of covariance differentiated sources of variation in the control variable measures and made adjustments for the differences in variation by compensating for them in the dependent variable measures. The mean scores of the dependent variable measures were then adjusted to account for initial differences within and between groups.

The statistic used with the analysis of covariance to determine the significance level for rejecting or accepting the null hypothesis was the F-value. The level chosen for rejecting the null hypothesis in this study was .05.

Teacher Responses.--The responses of teachers to the two questions on the Teacher Evaluation Form were detailed as a part of the analysis. Their responses were incorporated into the discussions of the hypotheses for which they seemed appropriate.

Summary

In this chapter the design and methodology for the study were described. The research design selected was the pretest-posttest control group design.

The setting for the enrichment tutorial experience was an inner-city school located in a large Midwestern industrial city. Adult volunteers were recruited to serve in the capacity of enrichment tutors. The sample selected for participation in enrichment tutoring contained male underachievers from the second, third and fourth grades. The treatment involved the enrichment tutors and the pupils assigned to them in pupil-oriented relationships. Enrichment and tutorial tasks were undertaken that related to the needs of the pupils.

Instruments designed to assess self-concept, educational achievement and measured intelligence were administered prior to and after treatment. At the close of the program teachers completed a questionnaire evaluating the effectiveness of the program.

Thirty-three statistical hypotheses concerned with self-concept, educational achievement and measured intelligence were generated and tested. The procedures used to analyze the data were the analysis of covariance for the statistical treatment of data and a listing of the teachers responses delineating their opinions regarding the effectiveness of the program.

[1]Carter V. Good, A. S. Barr and Douglas E. Scates, *The Methodology of Educational Research* (New York: Appleton-Century-Crofts, Inc., 1941), pp. 225-226.

[2]*Ibid.*, pp. 493-500.

[3]Donald T. Campbell and Julian C. Stanley, *Experimental and Quasi-Experimental Designs for Research* (Chicago: Rand McNally and Co., 1963), pp. 13-24.

[4]*Ibid.*, p. 2.

[5]J. Francis Rummel, *An Introduction to Research Procedures in Education* (New York: Harper and Row, Publishers, 1964), p. 196.

[6]See Appendix A.

[7]John E. Freund, *Modern Elementary Statistics* (Englewood Cliffs, New Jersey: Prentice-Hall, Inc., 1967), pp. 191-192.

[8]Norman K. Henderson, *Statistical Research Methods* (Hong Kong: Hong Kong University Press, 1964), p. 71.

[9]W. James Popham, *Educational Statistics* (New York: Harper and Row, Publishers, 1967), pp. 221-256.

[10]Ketcham and Morse, *op. cit.*, pp. 76-77.

[11]William C. Morse, "Administration and Scoring Procedures for Self-Esteem Inventory" (a mimeographed copy enclosed in a personal correspondence of January 29, 1968).

[12]Coopersmith, *loc. cit.*

[13]Morse, *loc. cit.*

[14]Coopersmith, *loc. cit.*

[15]Calvin O. Dyer, "Construct Validity of Self-Concept by a Multitrait-Multimethod Analysis" (unpublished Ph.D. Dissertation, University of Michigan, 1963).

[16]Ernest W. Tiegs and Willis W. Clark, *Manual: California Achievement Tests Complete Battery, Forms W and X, Lower Primary* (Monterey, California: California Test Bureau, 1963).

[17]Ernest W. Tiegs and Willis W. Clark, *Manual: California Achievement Tests Complete Battery, Forms W and X, Upper Primary* (Monterey, California: California Test Bureau, 1963).

[18]Elizabeth T. Sullivan, Willis W. Clark, and Ernest W. Tiegs, *Examiner's Manual: California Short-Form Test of Mental*

Maturity, Level 1 (Monterey, California: California Test Bureau, 1963).

[19]Elizabeth T. Sullivan, Willis W. Clark, and Ernest W. Tiegs, *Examiner's Manual: California Short-Form Test of Mental Maturity, Level 1H* (Monterey, California: California Test Bureau, 1964).

[20]*Ibid.*, p. 25.

[21]California Test Bureau, *Technical Report on the California Test of Mental Maturity Series* (Monterey, California: California Test Bureau, 1964).

[22]Gordon, Curran and Avila, *op. cit.*, pp. 111-116.

[23]Campbell and Stanley, *op. cit.*, p. 23.

[24]Walter R. Borg, *Educational Research* (New York: David McKay Company, Inc., 1963), pp. 143, 144.

[25]Popham, *loc. cit.*

CHAPTER 4

ANALYSIS OF THE EXPERIMENTAL DATA

In Chapter IV the findings which resulted from the analysis of the experimental data are reported. A primary research hypothesis and two subsidiary research hypotheses relating to self-concept, educational achievement and measured intelligence, respectively, were stated in Chapter I. The analysis of data is presented in the following manner: (1) analysis of the self-concept data; (2) analysis of the educational achievement data; and (3) analysis of the measured intelligence data.

For each of the research hypotheses, a major statistical hypothesis and several statistical subhypotheses are tested. One major statistical hypothesis and three statistical subhypotheses are tested in the area of self-concept. In addition to the major statistical hypothesis for educational achievement, three statistical subhypotheses concerned with achievement are inspected. In the area of measured intelligence, one major statistical hypothesis and two statistical subhypotheses are considered. Each of the hypotheses is investigated at the second-, third- and fourth-grade levels. In all, 33 statistical hypotheses are developed and tested. The analysis of covariance is the method of analysis utilized to test each hypothesis. The level of significance for rejecting a null hypothesis is established at .05.

Teacher opinions, as reported by responses to items included on the Teacher Evaluation Form, are analyzed with respect to participating pupils' self-concept development and educational achievement.

Analysis of the Self-Concept Data

The analysis of the self-concept data is presented in two parts. The first part involves the tests of the 12 statistical hypotheses relating to self-concept. The second part includes an analysis of the Teacher Evaluation Form responses which are related to self-concept.

Statistical Hypotheses Relating to Self-Concept.--The primary research hypothesis, which predicted the effects of enrichment tutoring on the self-concepts of underachieving pupils, was converted into one major statistical hypothesis and three statistical subhypotheses. The major statistical hypothesis was concerned with composite self-concept as related by the complete Coopersmith Self-Esteem Inventory (CSEI) scale. The subhypotheses were concerned with self-concept as related by the self subscale of the CSEI; social self-concept as related by the social self subscale of the CSEI; and the school self-concept as related by the school self subscale of the CSEI. The raw scores from the CSEI were used for the comparisons of experimental and control groups.

The null and alternate forms of Major Statistical Hypothesis 1 were:

Null Hypothesis 1: No difference will be found between tutored and non-tutored groups for composite self-concept as measured by average CSEI performance.

$$Ho_1: \quad M_1 = M_2$$

Alternate Hypothesis 1: The tutored group mean score for the composite self-concept of the CSEI will exceed that of the non-tutored group.

$$Ha_1: \quad M_1 > M_2$$

The null and alternate forms of Statistical Subhypothesis 11 were:

Null Hypothesis 11: No difference will be found between tutored and non-tutored groups on the self-concept subscale as measured by average CSEI performance.

$$Ho_{11}: \quad M_1 = M_2$$

Alternate Hypothesis 11: The tutored group mean score on the self-concept subscale of the CSEI will exceed that of the non-tutored group.

$$Ha_{11}: \quad M_1 > M_2$$

The null and alternate forms of Statistical Subhypothesis 12 were:

Null Hypothesis 12: No difference will be found between tutored and non-tutored groups on the social self-concept subscale as measured by average CSEI performance.

$$Ho_{12}: \quad M_1 = M_2$$

Alternate Hypothesis 12: The tutored group mean score on the social self-concept subscale of the CSEI will exceed that of the non-tutored group.

66

$$\text{Ha}_{12}: \quad M_1 > M_2$$

The null and alternate forms of Statistical Subhypothesis 13 were:

Null Hypothesis 13: No difference will be found between tutored and non-tutored groups on the school self-concept subscale as measured by average CSEI performance.

$$\text{Ho}_{13}: \quad M_1 = M_2$$

Alternate Hypothesis 13: The tutored group mean score on the school self-concept subscale of the CSEI will exceed that of the non-tutored group.

$$\text{Ha}_{13}: \quad M_1 > M_2$$

An analysis of covariance was computed for each of the statistical hypotheses at grade levels two, three and four. The results of the analyses of the self-concept data are reported in Tables 4.1 through 4.3.

The mean gains exhibited in Table 4.1 seemingly indicated, with one exception, positive gains favoring the experimental group. However, analyses of covariance for the hypotheses revealed no significant differences for any of the comparisons.

An F value of 4.38 was necessary for 1, 19 degrees of freedom before significant differences between the experimental and control groups could be claimed at the .05 level of significance. F values of less than 1.00 were found for each of the hypotheses tested at the second-grade level. Therefore, any differences between the groups may have occurred by chance. The null hypotheses, which stated there were no differences between tutored and non-tutored groups for composite self-concept, self-concept, social self-concept and school self-concept at the second-grade level, were not rejected.

The mean gains exhibited in Table 4.2 seemingly indicated, with one exception, positive gains favoring the control group. However, analyses of covariance for the hypotheses revealed that no significant differences between the groups with regard to self-concept existed.

An F value of 4.60 was necessary for 1, 14 degrees of freedom before significant differences between the experimental and control groups could be claimed at the .05 level of significance. F values of less than 3.60 were found for each of the hypotheses tested at the third-grade level. Therefore, any differences between the groups may have occurred by chance. The null hypotheses,

TABLE 4.1.--Results of the analyses of covariance for the data from the CSEI for the second-grade experimental and control groups.

Hypothesis	Mean*	Experimental Group (n = 11)	Control Group (n = 11)	Mean Gain**	Value of F	Null Hypothesis Was:
Ho_1	A	28.27	27.45	.36	.54	not rejected
	B	30.45	29.27			
	C	30.48	29.24			
Ho_{11}	A	17.36	16.82	.19	.65	not rejected
	B	17.91	17.18			
	C	17.99	17.10			
Ho_{12}	A	5.27	5.36	.27	.08	not rejected
	B	5.91	5.73			
	C	5.90	5.74			
Ho_{13}	A	5.64	5.27	-.15	.06	not rejected
	B	6.64	6.36			
	C	6.58	6.42			

*Legend for Means: A=Pretest Mean; B=Posttest Mean; and C=Adjusted Mean.

**Mean Gain = Experimental Gain - Control Gain.

which stated there were no differences between tutored and non-tutored groups for composite self-concept, self-concept, social self-concept and school self-concept at the third-grade level, were not rejected.

Mean gains exhibited in Table 4.3 for hypothesis Ho_1 and Ho_{12} seemingly favored the experimental group; while mean gains for Ho_{11} and Ho_{13} seemingly favored the control group. However, analyses of covariance for the hypotheses revealed that only one hypothesis, Ho_{12}, was rejected.

An F value of 4.41 was necessary with 1, 18 degrees of freedom before significant differences between the experimental and control groups could be claimed at the .05 level of significance. F values of less than 1.00 were found for Ho_1, Ho_{11} and Ho_{13} at the fourth-grade level. Therefore, the differences in composite self-concept, self-concept and school self-concept may have occurred by chance. The null hypotheses, which stated there were no differences between experimental and control groups for composite self-concept, self-concept and school self-concept at the

TABLE 4.2.--Results of the analyses of covariance for the data from the CSEI for the third-grade experimental and control groups.

Hypothesis	Mean*	Experimental Group (n = 9)	Control Group (n = 8)	Mean Gain**	Value of F	Null Hypothesis Was:
Ho_1	A	29.00	26.75	- .98	.14	not rejected
	B	31.89	30.62			
	C	31.61	30.93			
Ho_{11}	A	17.22	16.38	1.54	3.54	not rejected
	B	20.00	17.62			
	C	19.89	17.75			
Ho_{12}	A	6.11	5.50	-1.12	.94	not rejected
	B	6.00	6.50			
	C	5.99	6.51			
Ho_{13}	A	5.67	4.88	-1.40	1.94	not rejected
	B	5.89	6.50			
	C	5.74	6.67			

*Legend for Means: A = Pretest Mean; B = Posttest Mean; and C = Adjusted Mean.

**Mean Gain = Experimental Gain - Control Gain.

fourth-grade level, were not rejected.

Since an F value of 4.90 was determined for Ho_{12}, the hypothesis was rejected at the .05 level of significance. The differences between the experimental and control groups were not likely to have occurred by chance (differences as large as this would occur by chance less than five times in 100). Therefore, it can be assumed that enrichment tutoring did have an effect on the social self-concept development of the participating pupils at the fourth-grade level. The means of the tutored and non-tutored groups were found to be in accord with Ha_{12}. The tutored group mean exceeded the non-tutored group mean.

Teachers' Opinions Relating to Self-Concept.--Teachers' responses to Items One and Four of the Teacher Evaluation Form were analyzed in an effort to assess the effects of enrichment tutoring on the self-concept development of the participating pupils. Ten of the 11 participating teachers returned completed forms.

TABLE 4.3.--Results of the analyses of covariance for the data from the CSEI for the fourth-grade experimental and control groups.

Hypothesis	Mean*	Experimental Group (n = 11)	Control Group (n = 11)	Mean Gain**	Value of F	Null Hypothesis Was:
Ho_1	A	27.90	27.73	.68	.10	not rejected
	B	28.40	27.55			
	C	28.34	27.60			
Ho_{11}	A	17.50	15.91	-2.05	.98	not rejected
	B	16.90	17.36			
	C	16.32	17.89			
Ho_{12}	A	4.70	6.45	2.96	4.90	rejected
	B	6.30	5.09			
	C	6.73	4.70			
Ho_{13}	A	5.70	5.36	- .23	.01	not rejected
	B	5.20	5.09			
	C	5.17	5.12			

*Legend for Means: A = Pretest Mean; B = Posttest Mean; and C = Adjusted Mean.

**Mean Gain = Experimental Gain - Control Gain.

Four of the 10 teachers responded to Item One, "The most noteworthy aspects of the Educational Enrichment Program were _____," in a manner which could be related to self-concept. Some examples of teacher responses were:

"Gave children greater self-confidence."

"Positive change in self-concept."

In response to Item Four, "Do you feel the Educational Enrichment Program assisted the children assigned to it?" all 10 teachers responded with a "yes" reply. In addition, the item contained a second part which stated, "Explain the reason for your answer." Seven of the 10 teachers responded to the latter statement. Some examples of their responses related to self-concept were:

"Experience helped them gain self-confidence."

"Program gave pupils a feeling of importance."

"Self-attitudes of pupils seemed to change."

Analysis of the Educational Achievement Data

The analysis of the educational achievement data is reported in two parts. The first part involves the tests of 12 statistical hypotheses relating to educational achievement. The second part includes an analysis of the Teacher Evaluation Form responses which are related to educational achievement.

Statistical Hypotheses Relating to Educational Achievement.-- A secondary research hypothesis, which predicted the effects of enrichment tutoring on the educational achievement of underachieving pupils, was converted into one major statistical hypothesis and three statistical subhypotheses. The major statistical hypothesis was concerned with total educational achievement as related by total achievement on the California Achievement Test (CAT). The subhypotheses were concerned with reading achievement as related by the reading subtest of the CAT; arithmetic achievement as related by the arithmetic subtest of the CAT; and language achievement as related by the language subtest of the CAT. Raw scores from the CAT were converted to grade level equivalents and comparisons between the experimental and control groups at the second-, third- and fourth-grade levels were made.

The null and alternate forms of Major Statistical Hypothesis 2 were:

Null Hypothesis 2: No difference will be found between tutored and non-tutored groups for total educational achievement as measured by average CAT performance.

$$Ho_2: \quad M_1 = M_2$$

Alternate Hypothesis 2: The tutored group mean score for total educational achievement on the CAT will exceed that of the non-tutored group.

$$Ha_2: \quad M_1 > M_2$$

The null and alternate forms of Statistical Subhypothesis 21 were:

Null Hypothesis 21: No difference will be found between tutored and non-tutored groups for reading achievement as measured by average CAT performance.

$$Ho_{21}: \quad M_1 = M_2$$

Alternate Hypothesis 21: The tutored group mean score for reading achievement on the CAT will exceed that of the non-tutored group.

$$Ha_{21}: \quad M_1 > M_2$$

The null and alternate forms of Statistical Subhypothesis 22 were:

Null Hypothesis 22: No difference will be found between tutored and non-tutored groups for arithmetic achievement as measured by average CAT performance.

$$Ho_{22}: \quad M_1 = M_2$$

Alternate Hypothesis 22: The tutored group mean score for arithmetic achievement on the CAT will exceed that of the non-tutored group.

$$Ha_{22}: \quad M_1 > M_2$$

The null and alternate forms of Statistical Subhypothesis 23 were:

Null Hypothesis 23: No difference will be found between tutored and non-tutored groups for language achievement as measured by average CAT performance.

$$Ho_{23}: \quad M_1 = M_2$$

Alternate Hypothesis 23: The tutored group mean score for language achievement on the CAT will exceed that of the non-tutored group.

$$Ha_{23}: \quad M_1 > M_2$$

An analysis of covariance was run for each of the statistical hypotheses at grade levels two, three and four. The results of analyses of the educational achievement data are reported in Tables 4.4 through 4.6.

The mean gains exhibited in Table 4.4 seemingly indicated, with one exception, positive gains favoring the experimental group. However, analyses of covariance computed for the hypotheses showed significant differences to exist for only Ho_{23}. This hypothesis was concerned with language achievement.

An F value of 4.38 was necessary with 1, 19 degrees of free-

TABLE 4.4.--Results of the analyses of covariance for the data from the CAT for the second-grade experimental and control groups.

Hypothesis	Mean*	Experimental Group (n = 11)	Control Group (n = 11)	Mean Gain**	Value of F	Null Hypothesis Was:
Ho_2	A	1.32	1.28	.09	1.04	not rejected
	B	1.74	1.61			
	C	1.72	1.63			
Ho_{21}	A	1.21	1.15	.00	.12	not rejected
	B	1.61	1.55			
	C	1.56	1.60			
Ho_{22}	A	1.51	1.35	.12	.00	not rejected
	B	1.90	1.72			
	C	1.81	1.81			
Ho_{23}	A	1.13	1.35	.36	8.54	rejected
	B	1.73	1.59			
	C	1.80	1.52			

*Legend for Means: A = Pretest Mean; B = Posttest Mean; and C = Adjusted Mean.

**Mean Gain = Experimental Gain - Control Gain.

dom before significant differences between the experimental and control groups could be claimed at the .05 level of significance. F values of less than 1.10 were found for Ho_2, Ho_{21} and Ho_{22} at the second-grade level. Therefore, the differences in total educational achievement, reading achievement and arithmetic achievement may have occurred by chance. The null hypotheses, which stated there were no differences between tutored and non-tutored groups for total educational achievement, reading achievement and arithmetic achievement at the second-grade level, were not rejected.

Since an F value of 8.54 was determined for Ho_{23}, the hypothesis was rejected at the .05 level of significance. [23] The differences between the experimental and control groups were not likely to have occurred by chance. Therefore, it can be assumed that enrichment tutoring did have an effect on language achievement of the participating pupils at the second-grade level. The means of the tutored and non-tutored groups were found to be in accord with Ha_{23}. The tutored group mean exceeded the mean of the non-tutored group.

TABLE 4.5.--Results of the analyses of covariance for the data from the $\underline{CAT}$ for the third-grade experimental and control groups.

Hypothesis	Mean*	Experimental Group (n = 9)	Control Group (n = 8)	Mean Gain**	Value of F	Null Hypothesis Was:
Ho_2	A	2.30	2.18	.11	1.16	not rejected
	B	2.98	2.75			
	C	2.92	2.81			
Ho_{21}	A	2.18	1.82	.15	2.63	not rejected
	B	2.86	2.35			
	C	2.74	2.48			
Ho_{22}	A	2.30	2.50	.32	5.46	rejected
	B	3.18	3.06			
	C	3.27	2.96			
Ho_{23}	A	2.26	1.68	-.13	.04	not rejected
	B	2.69	2.24			
	C	2.50	2.45			

*Legend for Means: A = Pretest Mean; B = Posttest Mean; and C = Adjusted Mean.

**Mean Gain = Experimental Gain - Control Gain.

The mean gains exhibited in Table 4.5 seemingly indicated, with one exception, positive gains favoring the experimental group. However, analyses of covariance completed for the hypotheses indicated significant differences existed only for Ho_{22}. This hypothesis was concerned with arithmetic achievement.

An F value of 4.60 was necessary with 1, 14 degrees of freedom before significant differences between the experimental and control groups could be claimed at the .05 level of significance. F values of less than 2.70 were found for hypotheses Ho_2, Ho_{21} and Ho_{23} at the third-grade level. Therefore, the differences in total educational achievement, reading achievement and language achievement may have occurred by chance. The null hypotheses, which stated there were no differences between tutored and non-tutored groups for total educational achievement, reading achievement and language achievement at the third-grade level, were not rejected.

Since the F value of 5.46 was found for Ho_{22}, the hypothesis was rejected at the .05 level of significance. The differences between the groups were not likely to have occurred by chance. Therefore, it was assumed enrichment tutoring did have an effect on arithmetic achievement of the participating pupils at the third-grade level. The means of the tutored and non-tutored groups were found to be in accord with Ha_{22}. The tutored groups mean exceeded the mean of the non-tutored group.

The mean gains exhibited in Table 4.6 seemingly indicated, with one exception, positive gains that favored the experimental group. However, analyses of covariance were computed for the hypotheses which indicated there were no significant differences between the experimental and control groups.

An F value of 4.41 was necessary with 1, 18 degrees of freedom before significant differences could be claimed at the .05

TABLE 4.6.--Results of the analyses of covariance for the data from the CAT for the fourth-grade experimental and control groups.

Hypothesis	Mean*	Experimental Group (n = 10)	Control Group (n = 11)	Mean Gain**	Value of F	Null Hypothesis Was:
Ho_2	A	2.87	2.78	.09	.55	not
	B	3.16	2.98			rejected
	C	3.11	3.03			
Ho_{21}	A	2.59	2.65	-.13	.98	not
	B	2.85	3.04			rejected
	C	2.87	3.01			
Ho_{22}	A	3.15	2.95	.15	1.15	not
	B	3.36	3.01			rejected
	C	3.28	3.08			
Ho_{23}	A	2.27	2.36	.12	.19	not
	B	3.03	3.00			rejected
	C	3.07	2.97			

*Legend for Means: A = Pretest Mean; B = Posttest Mean; and C = Adjusted Mean.

**Mean Gain = Experimental Gain - Control Gain.

level of significance. F values of less than 1.20 were found for each of the hypotheses tested at the fourth-grade level. Therefore, the differences may have occurred by chance. The null hypotheses, which stated there were no differences between tutored and non-tutored groups for total educational achievement, reading achievement, mathematic achievement and language achievement at the fourth-grade level, were not rejected.

Teachers' Opinions Relating to Educational Achievement.--Teachers' responses to Items One and Four of the Teachers Evaluation Form were analyzed in an effort to assess the effects of enrichment tutoring on the educational achievement of the participating pupils.

Six of the 10 teachers responded to Item One, "The most trustworthy aspects of the Educational Enrichment Program were _____," in a manner which could be related to educational achievement. Examples of their replies were:

> "Seemed to have given pupils new outlooks about school work."

> "Increased interest in learning."

In response to Item Four, an item that related to how the Educational Enrichment Program assisted the participating pupils, some of the 10 replied in a manner which could be associated with educational achievement. Some of their responses were:

> "Improved pupils' reading."

> "Improvement in pupils' grades."

> "Increased interest in studies."

Analysis of the Measured Intelligence Data

A secondary research hypothesis, which predicted the effects of enrichment tutoring on the measured intelligence of underachieving pupils, was cast into one major statistical hypothesis and two statistical subhypotheses. The major statistical hypothesis was concerned with the total measured intelligence of pupils as indicated by the total battery. The statistical subhypotheses were concerned with the language intelligence of the pupils as measured by the language subtest of the California Short-Form Test of Mental Maturity (CTMM) and the non-language intelligence of the pupils as measured by the non-language intelligence subtest of the CTMM. Raw scores from the CTMM were converted to I.Q. equivalents and comparisons were made between experimental and control groups at the second-, third- and fourth-grade levels.

The null and alternate forms of Major Statistical Hypothesis 3 were:

Null Hypothesis 3: No difference will be found between
    tutored and non-tutored groups for total measured
    intelligence as measured by average CTMM perform-
    ance.

$$Ho_3: \quad M_1 = M_2$$

Alternate Hypothesis 3: The tutored group mean score
    for total measured intelligence on the CTMM will
    exceed that of the non-tutored group.

$$Ha_3: \quad M_1 > M_2$$

The null and alternate forms of Statistical Subhypothesis 31
were:

Null Hypothesis 31: No difference will be found between
    tutored and non-tutored groups for language measured
    intelligence as measured by average CTMM performance.

$$Ho_{31}: \quad M_1 = M_2$$

Alternate Hypothesis 31: The tutored group mean score
    for language measured intelligence on the CTMM will
    exceed that of the non-tutored group.

$$Ha_{31}: \quad M_1 > M_2$$

The null and alternate forms of Statistical Subhypothesis 32
were:

Null Hypothesis 32: No difference will be found between
    tutored and non-tutored groups for non-language
    measured intelligence as measured by average CTMM
    performance.

$$Ho_{32}: \quad M_1 = M_2$$

Alternate Hypothesis 32: The tutored group mean score
    for non-language measured intelligence on the CTMM
    will exceed that of the non-tutored group.

$$Ha_{32}: \quad M_1 > M_2$$

An analysis of covariance was run for each of the statistical
hypotheses at grade levels two, three and four. The results of
the analysis of the measured intelligence data are reported in
Tables 4.7 through 4.9.

TABLE 4.7.--Results of the analyses of covariance for the data from the CTMM for the second-grade experimental and control groups.

Hypothesis	Mean*	Experimental Group (n = 11)	Control Group (n = 11)	Mean Gain**	Value of F	Null Hypothesis Was:
Ho_3	A	85.64	86.09	2.26	.50	not
	B	89.36	87.55			rejected
	C	89.51	87.40			
Ho_{31}	A	86.18	87.91	3.18	1.05	not
	B	89.18	87.73			rejected
	C	89.89	87.01			
Ho_{32}	A	88.00	86.82	.36	.05	not
	B	92.18	90.64			rejected
	C	91.88	90.94			

*Legend for Means: A = Pretest Mean; B = Posttest Mean; C = Adjusted Mean.

**Mean Gain = Experimental Gain - Control Gain

The mean gains exhibited in Table 4.7 seemingly indicated positive gains favoring the experimental group. However, analysis of covariance tests were computed for the hypotheses and none of the tests revealed significant differences between the experimental and control groups.

An F value of 4.38 was necessary with 1,19 degrees of freedom before significant differences between the experimental and control groups could be claimed at the .05 level of significance. F values of less than 1.10 were found for each of the hypotheses tested. Therefore, the differences in total measured intelligence, language intelligence and non-language intelligence may have occurred by chance. The null hypotheses, which stated there were no differences between tutored and non-tutored groups for total measured intelligence, language intelligence and non-language intelligence at the second-grade level, were not rejected.

The mean gains exhibited in Table 4.8 seemingly indicated, with one exception, positive gains favoring the experimental group. However, analyses of covariance tests were computed for the hypotheses, and none of the tests revealed significant differences between the experimental and control groups.

An F value of 4.60 was necessary with 1,14 degrees of freedom before significant differences between the experimental and con-

TABLE 4.8.--Results of the analyses of covariance for the data from the <u>CTMM</u> for the third-grade experimental and control groups.

Hypothesis	Mean*	Experi- mental Group (n = 9)	Control Group (n = 8)	Mean Gain**	Value of F	Null Hypothesis Was:
Ho_3	A	,75.33	86.12	5.50	.00	not
	B	87.33	93.62			rejected
	C	90.19	90.41			
Ho_{31}	A	73.67	87.88	6.38	2.29	not
	B	86.67	94.50			rejected
	C	93.13	87.23			
Ho_{32}	A	83.67	87.12	-.30	.36	not
	B	91.00	94.75			rejected .
	C	91.53	94.15			

*Legend for Means: A = Pretest Mean; B = Posttest Mean; and
                     C = Adjusted Mean.

**Mean Gain = Experimental Gain - Control Gain.

trol groups could be claimed at the .05 level of significance. F values of less than 2.30 were found for each of the hypotheses tested at the third-grade level. Therefore, the differences found in total measured intelligence, language intelligence and non-language intelligence may have occurred by chance. The null hypotheses, which stated there were no differences between tutored and non-tutored groups for total measured intelligence, language intelligence and non-language intelligence at the third-grade level, were not rejected.

The mean gains exhibited in Table 4.9 seemingly indicated gains favoring the control group. However, analysis of covariance tests were computed for the hypotheses, and none of the tests revealed significant differences between the experimental and control groups.

An F value of 4.41 was necessary with 1, 18 degrees of freedom before significant differences could be claimed at the .05 level of significance. F values of less than 1.10 were found for each of the hypotheses tested. Therefore, the differences in the total measured intelligence, language intelligence and non-language intelligence may have occurred by chance. The null hypotheses, which stated there were no differences between tutored and non-tutored groups for total measured intelligence, language in-

TABLE 4.9.--Results of the analyses of covariance for the data from the CTMM for the fourth-grade experimental and control groups.

Hypothesis	Mean*	Experimental Group (N = 10)	Control Group (n = 11)	Mean Gain**	Value of F	Null Hypothesis Was:
Ho_3	A	82.80	83.09	-3.92	.38	not rejected
	B	76.00	80.27			
	C	76.66	80.22			
Ho_{31}	A	83.40	87.91	- .63	.26	not rejected
	B	78.30	82.18			
	C	78.80	81.73			
Ho_{32}	A	87.30	82.91	-7.83	1.05	not rejected
	B	81.20	84.64			
	C	79.87	85.84			

*Legend for Means: A = Pretest Mean; B = Posttest Mean; and C = Adjusted Mean.

**Mean Gain = Experimental Gain - Control Gain.

telligence and non-language intelligence at the fourth-grade level, were not rejected.

Summary

This experiment was designed to test the effectiveness of enrichment tutoring on the self-concept, the educational achievement and the measured intelligence of underachieving pupils in an inner-city elementary school. There were three treatment groups: one each at the second-, third- and fourth-grade levels.

Thirty-three statistical hypotheses were derived from the three research hypotheses. Four statistical hypotheses which related to self-concept were tested at each grade level. Twelve statistical hypotheses relating to composite self-concept, self-concept, school self-concept and social self-concept were tested. Four statistical hypotheses which related to educational achievement were tested at each grade level. Twelve statistical hypotheses related to total educational achievement, reading achievement, arithmetic achievement and language achievement were tested. Three statistical hypotheses which were related to measured intelligence were tested at each grade level. Nine hypotheses related to measured intelligence, language intelligence and non-language intelligence were tested.

The method used to test the null hypotheses of this study was the analysis of covariance. The F values derived from analysis of covariance tests were used to determine the significance level. The .05 level of significance was chosen for rejecting the null hypotheses.

Of the 33 null hypotheses tested, 30 were not rejected. Three were rejected. Differences were found to exist between the experimental and control groups in the following areas: (1) at the fourth-grade level, the social self-concepts of the tutored group were found to be significantly more positive after treatment than those of the non-tutored group; (2) at the second-grade level, the language achievement of the tutored group was found to be significantly higher after treatment than that of the non-tutored group; and (3) at the third-grade level, the tutored group exhibited significantly higher arithmetic performance after treatment than did the non-tutored group. No significant differences were found in measured intelligence.

Teacher responses on the Teacher Evaluation Form seemed to indicate positive changes in self-concept and educational achievement had resulted from enrichment tutoring.

CHAPTER 5

SUMMARY, CONCLUSIONS AND IMPLICATIONS
FOR FUTURE STUDY

The final chapter of this study is organized as follows:
(1) Summary; (2) Conclusions; and (3) Implications for future
study.

Summary

There were two purposes for this exploratory study. The
primary purpose was to investigate the effects of enrichment tutoring upon (1) self-concept, (2) educational achievement and (3)
measured intelligence of male underachievers in an inner-city
elementary school. A secondary purpose was to assess the effectiveness of enrichment tutoring as viewed by the participating
teachers in the school.

Treatment involved the assignment of volunteer enrichment
tutors to work with underachieving pupils in areas of academic
and enrichment needs. The tutors worked with pupils in an empha-
tic and understanding manner, yet expected and encouraged pupils
to strive to perform in accord with their individual potential.
Through several community agencies, 32 adults were recruited to
serve as enrichment tutors.

Sixty-five second-, third- and fourth-grade male pupils were
defined for possible participation in the enrichment tutorial program. Those selected as possible participants were pupils who had
been identified as underachievers by their classroom teachers and
who, in addition, scored two months or more below grade level on
the California Achievement Test. After identification, the pupils
were stratified by grade level and randomly assigned on a proportional basis by grade level to experimental and control groups.
At the outset 32 pupils were assigned to the experimental group
and 33 pupils were assigned to the control group. Movement from
the school district and placement in special educational situations resulted in two members of the experimental group and three
members of the control group being eliminated from the sample. At
the end of the six months' treatment period the total experimental
and total control groups each contained 30 members. At the second-grade level the experimental and control groups were composed
of 11 members each. The experimental group at the third-grade
level contained nine members, while the control group at the same
level contained eight members. At the fourth-grade level the experimental group was made up of 10 members and the membership in
the control group was composed of 11 pupils.

Changes in self-concept, educational achievement and measured intelligence were expected as a result of the treatment. The measures utilized to measure changes were, respectively: the Coopersmith Self-Esteem Inventory, the California Achievement Test and the California Short-Form Test of Mental Maturity. The instruments were administered to the experimental and control groups before and after treatment. The following primary research hypothesis was investigated:

H₁ The reported self-concept scores of inner-city elementary school male underachievers who experience enrichment tutoring will be more positive than the scores of inner-city elementary school male under-achievers who did not experience enrichment tutoring.

In addition the following subsidiary research hypotheses were investigated:

H₂ The educational achievement scores of inner-city elementary school male underachievers who experience enrichment tutoring will be more positive than the scores of inner-city elementary school male underachievers who did not experience enrichment tutoring.

H₃ The measured intelligence scores of inner-city elementary school male underachievers who experience enrichment tutoring will be more positive than the scores of inner-city elementary school male under-achievers who did not experience enrichment tutoring.

Since each instrument used to measure change reported a total score and several subscores for the variable measured, a major statistical hypothesis and several statistical subhypotheses were cast for each of the research hypotheses. A complete set of statistical hypotheses was cast at each grade level--two, three and four. The Coopersmith Self-Esteem Inventory included, in addition to the total score, subscores purported to measure self-concept, social self-concept and school self-concept. Besides the total grade level equivalent score reported by the California Achievement Test, grade level equivalents for reading, arithmetic and language achievement were also reported. The California Short-Form Test of Mental Maturity presented a total measured intelligence score which was composed of language and non-language intelligence factors. A total of three major statistical hypotheses and nine statistical subhypotheses were investigated for self-concept at the second-, third- and fourth-grade levels. The educational achievement data involved the investigation of three major statistical hypotheses and nine statistical subhypotheses at the second-, third- and fourth-grade levels. Three major statistical hypotheses and six statistical subhypotheses concerned with intelligence were investigated at the second-, third- and fourth-grade levels.

Statistical comparisons of the groups were accomplished by

analysis of covariance tests. F values were utilized to determine significance. The level of significance was placed at the .05 level for the purposes of this study. Only subjects who were involved in the total treatment period were included in the final analysis.

In addition to the statistical analysis, the reported opinions of teachers on the Teacher Evaluation Form were assessed to determine the effectiveness of enrichment tutoring. Only information which would relate to self-concept development and to educational achievement was reported by the teachers for the participating pupils.

Summary of the Findings.--The findings for the study are divided into two areas--(1) The analysis of the statistical data and (2) The analysis of teacher opinions as reported on the Teacher Evaluation Form.

The analysis of covariance tests used to test the null hypotheses for self-concept indicated the following:

1.   There were no significant differences between tutored and non-tutored groups for composite self-concept, self-concept, social self-concept or school self-concept as measured by the Coopersmith Self-Esteem Inventory at the second-grade level.

2.   There were no significant differences between tutored and non-tutored groups for composite self-concept, self-concept, social self-concept or school self-concept as measured by the Coopersmith Self-Esteem Inventory at the third-grade level.

3.   There were no significant differences between tutored and non-tutored groups for composite self-concept, self-concept or school self-concept as measured by the Coopersmith Self-Esteem Inventory at the fourth-grade level.

4.   Enrichment tutoring produced significant differences between tutored and non-tutored groups for social self-concept as measured by the Coopersmith Self-Esteem Inventory at the fourth-grade level. The differences were in the projected direction, that is, the direction favored the tutored group.

The analysis of covariance tests used to test the null hypotheses for achievement indicated the following:

5.   There were no significant differences between tutored and non-tutored groups for educational achievement, reading achievement or arithmetic achievement as measured by the California Achievement Test at the second-grade level.

6. Enrichment tutoring produced significant differences between tutored and non-tutored groups for language achievement as measured by the California Achievement Test at the second-grade level. The differences were in the projected direction, that is, the direction favored the tutored group.

7. There were no significant differences between tutored and non-tutored groups for educational achievement, reading achievement or language achievement as measured by the California Achievement Test at the third-grade level.

8. Enrichment tutoring produced significant differences between tutored and non-tutored groups for arithmetic achievement as measured by the California Achievement Test at the third-grade level. The differences were in the projected direction, that is, favored the tutored group.

9. There were no significant differences between tutored and non-tutored groups for educational achievement, reading achievement, arithmetic achievement or language achievement as measured by the California Achievement Test at the fourth-grade level.

The analysis of covariance tests used to test the null hypotheses for intelligence indicated the following:

10. There were no significant differences between tutored and non-tutored groups for measured intelligence, language intelligence or non-language intelligence as measured by the California Short-Form Test of Mental Maturity at the second-grade level.

11. There were no significant differences between tutored and non-tutored groups for measured intelligence, language intelligence or non-language intelligence as measured by the California Short-Form Test of Mental Maturity at the third-grade level.

12. There were no significant differences between tutored and non-tutored groups for measured intelligence, language intelligence or non-language intelligence as measured by the California Short-Form Test of Mental Maturity at the fourth-grade level.

Teachers subjectively responded to the Teacher Evaluation Form in the following manner:

13. Pupils who participated in enrichment tutoring: gained in self-confidence; exhibited a positive change in self-concept; and, felt more important.

14. Pupils who participated in enrichment tutoring: seemed

to have new outlooks about school work; had increased interest in learning; improved reading ability; and improved grades.

Conclusions

The literature related to the present study suggested that enrichment tutoring might improve the self-concept, the educational achievement and the measured intelligence of the participating underachievers. Though the results of the study do not lend empirical support to the theory underlying enrichment tutoring, the subjective opinions of teachers as reported in response to the evaluation form tend to emphasize growth in self-concept and educational achievement.

Of the 33 null hypotheses developed for the purposes of this study: three were rejected and 30 were not rejected. None of the major statistical hypotheses were rejected.

In the area of self-concept, three major null hypotheses were developed, none of which were rejected. Of the nine null subhypotheses tested, only one was rejected. The null subhypothesis concerned with social self-concept at the fourth-grade level was rejected. There was a difference favoring the tutored group, significant at the .05 level, for the social-self subscale.

Of the three major null hypotheses for educational achievement tested, none were rejected. Two null subhypotheses were rejected. At the second-grade level the null hypothesis concerned with language achievement was rejected. There was a difference favoring the tutored group, significant at the .05 level, for the subtest of language achievement. At the third-grade level the null hypothesis concerned with arithmetic achievement was rejected. There was a difference favoring the tutored group, significant at the .05 level, for the subtest of arithmetic achievement.

The three major null hypotheses related to measured intelligence were not rejected. In addition, the six null subhypotheses related to intelligence were not rejected.

Teachers reported positive changes in self-concept and educational achievement as a result of enrichment tutoring.

The general research hypotheses, H_1, H_2 and H_3, must be rejected. Overall, enrichment tutoring did not appear to significantly influence the composite self-concept, the total educational achievement or the total measured intelligence of the participating group. A closer examination of the data, however, leads to the following conclusions within the limitations noted in Chapter I:

1. No differences were found among tutored groups and non-tutored groups for total self-concept (composite self scale), self-concept (self-concept subscale) and

school self-concept (school self-subscale) at the second-, third- and fourth-grade levels. This was also true for social self-concept (social self-subscale) at the second- and third-grade levels.

2. No differences were found among tutored and non-tutored groups for total educational achievement (total achievement battery results) or reading achievement (reading subtest results) at the second-, third- or fourth-grade levels. Likewise, no differences were found among either tutored and non-tutored groups for arithmetic achievement (arithmetic subtest results) at the second- and fourth-grade levels or tutored and non-tutored groups for language achievement (language subtest results) at the third- and fourth-grade levels.

3. No differences were found among tutored and non-tutored groups on changes in total measured intelligence (total battery results), language intelligence (language subtest results) or non-language intelligence (non-language subtest) at the second-, third- or fourth-grade levels.

4. At the fourth-grade level, the tutored group positively and significantly exceeded the non-tutored group in social self-concept (social self subscale).

5. At the second-grade level, the tutored group positively and significantly exceeded the non-tutored group in language achievement (language subtest results).

6. At the third-grade level, the tutored group positively and significantly exceeded the non-tutored group in arithmetic achievement (arithmetic subtest results).

In addition, teacher reports led to the following conclusions:

7. Subjectively, teachers indicated positive changes in self-confidence, self-attitudes and the self-worth on the part of participating pupils.

8. Subjectively, teachers indicated improved study habits, improved grades and improved reading on the part of participating pupils.

Since this exploratory study was conducted at the second-, third- and fourth-grade levels in a single elementary school located in the inner-city, findings must be restricted to that school and others similar to it. No effort was made to make the sample representative of the general population of underachieving pupils. Through randomization an effort was made to equate the experimental and control groups at all grade levels. The method of analysis, the analysis of covariance, provided controls for initial group differences. The pretests were used for control purposes.

The foci of the study were the statistical comparisons of the experimental and control groups and the subjective opinions of teachers as reported in an evaluation of the enrichment tutorial program. Even though the findings and conclusions drawn from the statistical data of the study did not seem to support the general research hypotheses relating to self-concept, educational achievement and measured intelligence, further inspection of the data reveals that there are no apparent negative effects. In fact, the tests of the null hypotheses indicated that there were no significant differences for 30 hypotheses, while there were significant differences for three hypotheses favoring the experimental groups in areas of self-concept and achievement.

The subjective data reported by the participating classroom teachers seemed to be supportive of the research hypotheses for self-concept and educational achievement. Their reports implied that enrichment tutoring did have positive effects on the self-concept development and educational achievement of some of the participating pupils. It is possible that teachers' assessments of participating pupils reflected individual performances and probably excluded cases in which success failed to occur.

In view of both the statistical data and the subjective opinions of the participating teachers there does seem to be evidence that would indicate that some of the pupils who participated in enrichment tutoring made positive gains. Had the experimental and control groups been larger, it is possible that other significant differences might have been determined. The method of analysis used to test the null hypotheses demanded a greater margin of error when working with small groups.

Group comparisons were not possible using the members of the second-, third- and fourth-grade experimental and control groups as a whole. The measurement devices, with the exception of self-concept, used to measure changes in the groups were so constructed that different levels of the instruments were necessitated at the various grade levels. Since different levels of the instruments were used, comparisons between the total groups were unwarranted. In addition, comparisons between groups containing pupils from different grade levels might have confounded the data.

Since Negro pupils represented a majority of the memberships of both the experimental and control groups, the status of the Negro self-concept might have had a deleterious effect on the data. In the literature there are indications that the Negro self-concept is less than adequate.[1] Yet there is little recent objective support for this point of view. On the other hand, there is also literature that indicates this has been true in the past, but argues that the civil rights movement has had a positive effect on the Negro self-concept.[2] If the assumption that the Negro self-concept is less adequate than the self-concept of the majority white population is valid, then the data found at the second-grade level may be of questionable value. The 11 pupils who composed the membership of the experimental group were all minority group members, while two of the 11 members of the control group were members of the broader populace. At grade levels three and four, all members of the experimental and control groups were Negroes.

With regard to self-concept the objective data indicated little change as a result of enrichment tutoring. These findings are consistent with the findings of Brookover and associates who attempted to create significant others for underachieving pupils in secondary schools. By assigning counselors who held high expectations and evaluations of students to the members of an experimental group they hoped to show that the self-concept of ability of the participating members could be improved. The experiment was undertaken at the ninth-grade level. Through grade twelve no significant differences were found between the experimental and control groups.[3]

Gordon and associates at the University of Florida provided tutors for a group of underachieving pupils at the late elementary and junior high school levels. They reported no differences between experimental and control groups for measured self-concept as a result of the treatment.[4]

Ketcham and Morse indicated that "as children progress through the elementary and secondary grades their self-images . . . take on an increasingly negative quality."[5] The average composite self-concept scores found in the present study indicated that in every instance, save one, the experimental and control groups showed positive, but not necessarily significant gains during the treatment period. For one group, the control group at the fourth-grade level, a decrease was observed. The difference was very small and insignificant. The composite scores at grades two and three were higher than the composite scores at the fourth-grade level. At the fourth-grade level a positive and significant gain in social self-concept was indicated for the experimental group.

The opinions of participating teachers indicated that enrichment tutoring did have a positive effect on the self-concept development of some of the pupil participants. Perhaps individual case studies of the participating pupils would have added further information in this area. Gordon and associates found that teachers indicated positive changes in behavior for Negro pupils involved in a tutorial program. According to measured behavior changes, by teacher assessment, the pupils became less aggressive in their behavior. In addition, the teachers verbally indicated that pupils who participated in the program improved in their classroom behavior.[6]

Engle attempted to have "warm teachers" and "peer leaders" become significant others for underachieving secondary school pupils. Measures of the overt behavior of the experimental and control groups indicated: (1) the "warm teacher" experiment resulted in fewer teacher referrals for disciplinary action among the experimental group; and (2) the "peer leader" experiment resulted in fewer teacher referrals for disciplinary action and less tardiness for the experimental group.[7]

In this study in the achievement area, significant differences were indicated for two of the statistical analyses. These differences favored the experimental groups and were reported for language achievement at the second-grade level and arithmetic achievement at the third-grade level.

Studies of disadvantaged students might hold the key for understanding why changes occurred in language achievement favoring the experimental group at the second-grade level. Researchers who have studied language development in the homes of the disadvantaged have argued that the language patterns in these homes are detrimental to the child in school. In enrichment programs developed for children from these areas, it has been assumed that in these homes language development is limited and therefore emphasis has been given to programs that actively provide youngsters the opportunity to converse with and listen to adults.[8,9] Early intervention programs which have incorporated such ideas have been instrumental in improving I.Q. scores and verbal functions of disadvantaged children.[10] The advocates of these programs have emphasized that perhaps such programs should be followed through at higher grade levels.[11]

The differences in arithmetic achievement at the third-grade level could have resulted from more extensive drill. It would appear that if drill and practice in arithmetic were undertaken that changes in achievement favoring the experimental group would have followed since the arithmetic achievement tests utilized in the study emphasized computational skills at grade levels two, three and four. Yet, significant improvement was indicated only for the third-grade level. Perhaps this implies that the enrichment tutors at this grade level placed greater emphasis upon arithmetic drill and practice.

Teachers' opinions indicated that some pupils improved their total school work as a result of enrichment tutoring. Some teachers reported improved reading while others reported improved teacher-assigned grades.

Studies related to enrichment tutoring indicated improvement in achievement as resulting from the treatments. Baun[12] found that tutoring significantly improved the reading level of Negro pupils. Cloward[13] reported significant differences in reading achievement favoring a group of pupils who participated in a four-hour weekly tutorial session. At the secondary level Engle[14] reported improved achievement as measured by teacher grades as a result of assigning underachieving pupils to work with "peer leaders."

In this study, no significant differences were found between experimental and control groups for measured intelligence at any grade level. There was, however, a difference in the various grade levels that should be noted. At each grade level, except the fourth, the mean measured intelligence for the experimental and control groups were higher for the posttests than for the pretests. At the fourth-grade level the mean scores for the posttests were considerably lower than the mean scores for the pretests. This probably can be accounted for by the fact that the school district found it necessary to administer an achievement test during the week that the posttest for measured intelligence was administered. It is felt that the results for the fourth-grade groups were probably influenced by this test administration.

Teachers reported no results that were indicative of changes in measured intelligence.

Implications for Future Study

The results of this study and the evidence from the literature appear to imply that further study of enrichment tutoring is merited. Although the statistical trends did not generally support the research hypotheses, some positive trends were determined. The coupling of these trends with the positive teachers' evaluations from this and other programs related to enrichment tutoring give ample implications for the following questions for future study.

The present study was lacking in that the groups used for comparative purposes were relatively small. As a result, this question could be posed: If larger groups had been defined, would there have been more significant differences for the hypotheses tested?

Changes in self-concept, achievement, and intelligence are probably difficult to effect. The literature definitely emphasizes that changes in self-concept are difficult to bring about and that the improvement of achievement of underachieving students who have met with little success has been and is a formidable task. Further, it must be admitted that numerous questions exist concerning intelligence for those who have been deprived of opportunities. If changes are possible in these areas, probably they are gradual and this question must be asked: Should the treatment in this study have extended over a longer period of time?

The assessment of self-concept at the lower elementary levels is a questionable matter. Theoretically, measures are available to accurately assess achievement and intelligence at these levels. Studies related to tutoring completed at higher grade levels have shown success in areas of achievement. Would studies at higher grade levels have positive results in the areas of self-concept and intelligence?

Suppose enrichment tutoring did not result in immediate changes, but rather brings about gradual changes. This seems to be a possibility, at least in the area of self-concept. If more adequate self-concepts are associated with positive achievement, as suggested by some researchers of self-concept, then achievement change, accompanying gradual change in self-concept, would be gradual. Experience is closely associated with intelligence. Would changes in intelligence which accompany new experiences be gradual? Is a follow-up study in the future merited?

Pupils who were selected for possible participation in the experiment ranged from two months through two years and five months below grade level. The results from the study indicated few significant statistical differences. Had the sample of underachievers represented a group of more extreme underachievers, that is, one year or more below grade level, would the findings have differed?

In addition, the question must be asked: Does enrichment tutoring affect all segments of the population in the same manner? Are middle class, outer-city or suburban underachievers or underachievers from the general population affected in the same manner as inner-city underachievers?

Finally, the question could be posed: Did the subjective opinions of teachers actually reflect their attitudes with regard to the children who participated in enrichment tutoring? Would the results have been the same for another group of underachievers who the teachers were told received enrichment tutoring, but in reality did not? By the same token, did enrichment tutoring affect the attitudes teachers held with regard to participating pupils? If scales used to measure attitudes toward pupils had been administered to the teachers before and after treatment, would changes have been reflected?

From these questions the following recommendations for future research were evolved:

1.   Replication of this study is desirable to discover if other enrichment tutors working with similar pupils obtain the same results. Replication could demonstrate that the results were due to treatment effects and not the skills or the personalities of the tutors involved.

2.   Replication of the study with larger samples at all three grade levels, or for that matter any number of grade levels, is indicated since the possibility of significant results is much more likely with larger groups.

3.   Replication of the study with a considerably longer period of treatment is desirable to determine if longer periods of treatment result in improved self-concept, educational achievement and measured intelligence.

4.   Replication of this study with larger samples using the same basic approach, but applied at higher grade levels, is suggested to determine if enrichment tutoring has

similar effects at higher grade levels.

5. A follow-up study should be undertaken one year after treatment to determine the permanence of the self-concept and achievement gains noted and to determine if other changes have come about as a result of the treatment.

6. Replication of this study with a more extreme sample of underachievers is desirable to determine if the degree of underachievement is a factor which influences the findings.

7. A study should be undertaken pairing underachievers from an outer-city or suburban school or underachievers from the general population with underachievers from an inner-city school in an effort to compare the effects of enrichment tutoring on different types of under-achievers.

8. A study which involves an experimental group, a control group and a placebo group should be undertaken to determine teachers' attitudes with respect to enrichment tutoring and the participating pupils. Measures of teachers' attitudes regarding the pupils in the various groups could be taken before and after treatment, thereby permitting comparisons of the several groups. In this manner the effectiveness of enrichment tutoring could be determined as well as permitting a measure of change in teacher attitudes regarding children as a result of the treatment.

[1]William C. Kvaraceus, *The Negro Self-Concept* (New York: McGraw Hill, 1965), pp. 11-127.

[2]Michigan State University, *loc. cit.*

[3]Brookover, Erickson and Joiner, *op. cit.*, pp. 127-137.

[4]Gordon, Curran, and Avila, *op. cit.*, pp. 76-78.

[5]Ketcham and Morse, *op. cit.*, p. 204.

[6]Gordon, Curran, and Avila, *loc. cit.*

[7]Engle, *loc. cit.*

[8]Mariam L. Goldberg, "Factors Affecting Education Attainment in Depressed Urban Areas," *Education in Depressed Areas*, ed. A. Harry Passow (New York: Teachers' College, Columbia University, 1963), pp. 68-99.

[9]Martin Deutsch, "The Disadvantaged Child and the Learning Process," *op. cit.*, pp. 37-57.

[10]Cynthia P. Deutsch and Martin Deutsch, "Brief Reflections on the Theory of Early Childhood Enrichment Programs," *The Disadvantaged Child*, ed. Martin Deutsch (New York: Basic Books, Inc., 1967), pp. 379-387.

[11]*Ibid.*

[12]Baun, *loc. cit.*

[13]Cloward, *loc. cit.*

[14]Engle, *loc. cit.*

BIBLIOGRAPHY

Books

Ausubel, David P. *Theory and Problems of Child Development.* New York: Grune and Stratton, 1958.

Bass, Bernard M., and Irvin A. Bay, ed. *Objective Approaches to Personality Assessment.* Princeton, N. J.: D. Van Nostrand Company, 1959.

Bernard, Howard W. *Psychology of Learning and Teaching.* New York: McGraw-Hill Books, Inc., 1954.

Borg, Walter R. *Educational Research.* New York: David McKay Company, Inc., 1963.

Brookover, Wilbur B., Ann Patterson, and Shailer Thomas. *Self-Concept of Ability and School Achievement.* East Lansing, Michigan: Office of Research and Publications, Michigan State University, 1962.

_____, and David Gottlieb. *A Sociology of Education.* New York: American Book Company, 1964.

_____, Jean Lepere and others. *Self-Concept of Ability and School Achievement, II.* East Lansing, Michigan: Office of Research and Publications, Michigan State University, 1965.

_____, Edsel L. Erickson, and Lee M. Joiner. *Self-Concept of Ability and School Achievement, III.* East Lansing, Michigan: Office of Research and Publication, Michigan State University, 1967.

Campbell, Donald T., and Julian C. Stanley. *Experimental and Quasi-Experimental Designs for Research.* Chicago: Rand McNally and Co., 1963.

Chase, Clinton I., and H. Glenn Ludlow, ed. *Readings in Educational and Psychological Measurement.* Boston: Houghton-Mifflin Co., 1966.

Coleman, James S., and others. *Equality of Educational Opportunity.* Washington, D. C.: U. S. Office of Education, Government Printing Office, 1966.

Combs, Arthur W., ed. *Perceiving, Behaving, Becoming.* Washington, D. C.: Association for Supervision and Curriculum Development, National Education Association, 1962.

Cronbach, Lee J. *Educational Psychology*. New York: Harcourt, Brace and Co., 1954.

Deutsch, Martin, ed. *The Disadvantaged Child*. New York: Basic Books, Inc., 1967.

Dewey, John. Democracy and Education. New York: The MacMillen Co., 1916.

Freund, Janet. *Coordinator Guide*. Winnetka, Illinois: Winnetka Public Schools, 1966.

Freund, John E. *Modern Elementary Statistics*. Englewood Cliffs, New Jersey: Prentice-Hall, Inc., 1967.

Fullagar, William, and others, ed. *Readings for Educational Psychology*. New York: Thomas Y. Crowell Company, 1964.

Good, Carter V., A. S. Barr and Douglas E. Scates. *The Methodology of Educational Research*. New York: Appleton-Century-Crafts, Inc., 1941.

Gordon, Edmund W., and Doxey A. Wilkerson. *Compensatory Programs for the Disadvantaged*. New York: College Entrance Examination Board, 1966.

Gordon, Ira J. *Human Development: From Birth to Adolescence*. New York: Harper and Brothers, Inc., 1962.

_____, Robert L. Curran and Donald L. Avila. *An Inter-Disciplinary Approach to Improving the Development of Culturally Disadvantaged Children*. Gainsville, Florida: College of Education, University of Florida, 1966.

_____. *Studying the Child in School*. New York: John Wiley and Sons, Inc., 1966.

Hausdorf, Henry, Ed. *A.E.R.A. Paper Abstracts*. Washington, D. C.: American Educational Research Association, 1968.

Henderson, Norman K. *Statistical Research Methods*. Hong Kong: Hong Kong University Press, 1964.

Hunt, Joseph McV. *Intelligence and Experience*. New York: The Ronald Press Co., 1961.

James, William. *Psychology*. New York: Henry Holt and Co., 1892.

Janowitz, Gayle. *Helping Hands*. Chicago: University of Chicago Press, 1965.

Jersild, Arthur T. *Child Psychology*. Englewood Cliffs, New Jersey: Prentice Hall, Inc., 1960.

Ketcham, Warren A., and William C. Morse. *Dimensions of Chil-*

dren's Social and Psychological Development Related to School Achievement. Ann Arbor, Michigan: School of Education, University of Michigan, 1965.

Kvaraceus, William C., ed. *The Negro Self-Concept.* New York: McGraw-Hill, 1965.

Lecky, Prescott. *Self-Consistency: A Theory of Personality.* New York: Island Press, 1945.

Mead, George H. *Mind, Self and Society.* Chicago: The University of Chicago Press, 1934.

Michigan State University. *Proceeding of a Symposium: A symposium on School Integration.* East Lansing, Michigan: Bureau of Educational Research, Michigan State University, May, 1964.

Newcomb, T. M., and E. L. Hartley, ed. *Reading in Social Psychology.* New York: Holt, 1947.

Noce, James. *Research and Evaluation in Tutorial Programs.* Washington, D. C.: Tutorial Assistance Center, 2215 S. Street, N. W., 1967.

Passow, A. Harry, ed. *Education in Depressed Areas.* New York: Teachers College, Columbia University, 1963.

Popham, W. James. *Educational Statistics.* New York: Harper and Row, Publishers, 1967.

Roberts, Joan I., ed. *School Children in the Urban Slum.* New York: The Free Press, 1967.

Rogers, Carl R. *Client-Centered Therapy.* Boston: Houghton Mifflin Company, 1951.

_____. *On Becoming a Person.* Boston: Houghton Mifflin Company, 1961.

Rosenberg, Morris. *Society and the Adolescent Self-Image.* Princeton, New Jersey: Princeton University Press, 1965.

Rosenthal, Robert, and Lenore Jacobson. *Pygmalion in the Classroom.* New York: Holt, Rinehart and Winston, Inc., 1968.

Rummel, J. Francis. *An Introduction to Research Procedures in Education.* New York: Harper and Row, Publishers, 1964.

Sexton, Patricia C. *Education and Income.* New York: Viking Press, 1961.

Snygg, Donald, and Arthur W. Combs. *Individual Behavior.* New York: Harper and Row, Publishers, 1959.

Stephenson, William. *The Study of Behavior: Q-Technique and Its*

Methodology. Chicago: University of Chicago Press, 1953.

Sullivan, Harry S. *The Interpersonal Theory of Psychiatry*. New York: W. W. Norton and Company, Inc., 1953.

Trager, Helen, and Miriam Yarrow. *They Learn What They Live*. New York: Harpers, 1952.

Travers, Robert M. W. *Essentials of Learning*. New York: The MacMillan Company, 1963.

United States Commission on Civil Rights. *Racial Isolation in the Public Schools, Vol. I*. Washington, D. C.: U. S. Government Printing Office, 1967.

United States Commission on Civil Rights. *Racial Isolation in the Public Schools, Vol. II*. Washington, D. C.: U. S. Government Printing Office, 1967.

Waltzen, Walter, ed. *Learning and Mental Health in the School*. Washington, D. C.: Association for Supervision and Curriculum Development, N.E.A., 1966.

Wylie, Ruth. *The Self Concept*. Lincoln, Nebraska: University of Nebraska Press, 1961.

Periodicals

Asbell, Bernard. "The Case of the Wandering I.Q.'s." *Redbook*, 129 (1967), pp. 31-36.

Baldwin, Alfred L., Joan Kalhorn, and Fay H. Breese. "Patterns of Parent Behavior." *Psychological Monographs*, 58 (1945), pp. 1-75.

Baun, Eugene. "The Washington University Campus Y Tutoring Project." *Peabody Journal of Education*, 43 (1965), pp. 161-168.

Campbell, Clyde M. "The Educative Community." *The Community School and Its Administration*, 5 (May, 1967).

Carter, Howard A. "The Retired Senior Citizen as a Resource to Minimize Underachievement of Children in Public Schools." *Archives of Physical Medicine and Rehabilitation*, Vol. 35 (1964), pp. 218-223.

Cloward, Robert D. "The Nonprofessional in Education: Mobilization for Youth's Tutorial Project." *Educational Leadership*, 24 (1967), pp. 604-606.

Coopersmith, Stanley. "A Method for Determining Types of Self-Esteem." *Journal of Abnormal and Social Psychology*, 19 (1959), pp. 87-94.

Davids, Anthony, and Marcia J. Lawton. "Self-Concept, Mother-Concept and Food Aversion in Emotionally Disturbed and Normal Children." *Journal of Abnormal and Social Psychology*, 62 (1961), pp. 309-314.

Davidson, Helen H., and Gerhard Lang. "Children's Perceptions of Their Teachers' Feelings Toward Them Related to Self Perception, School Achievement and Behavior." *Journal of Experimental Education*, 29 (1960), pp. 107-118.

Dennis, Wayne. "Causes of Retardation Among Institutional Children: Iran." *Journal of Genetic Psychology*, 96 (1960), pp. 47-59.

Engel, Mary. "The Stability of Self-Concept in Adolescence." *Journal of Abnormal and Social Psychology*, 58 (1959), pp. 211-215.

Farquhar, William W., and David A. Payne. "A Classification of Techniques Used in Selecting Under- and Overachieving Students." *American Personnel and Guidance Journal*, 42 (1964), pp. 874-884.

Fink, Martin B. "Self-Concept As It Relates to Academic Underachievement." *California Journal of Educational Research*, 13 (1962), pp. 57-62.

Flanders, Ned A. "Personal-Social Anxiety as a Factor in Experimental Learning Situations." *Journal of Educational Research*, 45 (1951), pp. 100-110.

Freund, Janet. "Time and Knowledge to Share." *Elementary School Journal*, 65 (1965), pp. 351-358.

Green, Robert L., and William Farquhar. "Negro Academic Motivation and Scholastic Achievement." *Journal of Educational Psychology*, 56 (1965), pp. 241-243.

Johnson, David W. "Racial Attitudes of Negro Freedom School Participants and Negro and White Civil Rights Participants." *Social Forces*, 45 (1966), pp. 266-273.

Likert, Rensis. "A Technique for the Measurement of Attitudes." *Archives of Psychology*, 140 (1932), pp. 5-43.

Manis, Melvin. "Social Interaction and the Self-Concept." *Journal of Abnormal and Social Psychology*, 51 (1955), pp. 362-370.

McDavid, John. "Some Relationships Between Social Reinforcement and Scholastic Achievement." *Journal of Consulting Psychology*, 23 (1959), pp. 151-154.

Medinnus, Gene R. "Adolescents' Self Acceptance and Perception of Their Parents." *Journal of Consulting Psychology*, 29

(1965), pp. 150-154.

Raimy, Victor C. "Self-Reference in Counseling Intervention."
    Journal of Counseling Psychology, 12 (1948), pp. 153-156.

Shaw, Melville C., Kenneth Edson and Hugh Bell. "The Self-Con-
    cept of Bright Underachieving High School Students as Re-
    vealed by an Adjective Checklist." *Personnel and Guidance
    Journal*, 89 (1960), pp. 193-196.

Telego, Gene. "A Teen Tutorial Program." *Pacereport* (Lexington,
    Kentucky: A publication of the College of Education, Uni-
    versity of Kentucky, May-June, 1968), pp. 15-17.

Whitehorn, John C., and Barbara J. Betz. "A Study of Psycho-
    therapeutic Relationships Between Physicians and Schizo-
    phrenic Patients." *American Journal of Psychiatry*, 111
    (1954), pp. 321-331.

Unpublished Materials

Bodwin, Raymond F. "The Relationship Between Immature Self-Con-
    cept and Certain Educational Disabilities." Unpublished
    Ph.D. Dissertation, Michigan State University, 1957.

Bruck, Max. "A Study of Age Differences and Sex Differences in
    the Relationship Between Self-Concept and Grade-Point Aver-
    age." Unpublished Ph.D. Dissertation, Michigan State Uni-
    versity, 1957.

Butcher, Donald G. "A Study of the Relationships of Student Self-
    Concept to Academic Achievement in Six High Achieving Ele-
    mentary Schools." Unpublished Ed.D. Dissertation, Michigan
    State University, 1967.

Campbell, Paul B. "Self-Concept and Academic Achievement in
    Middle Grade Public School Children." Unpublished Ed.D.
    Dissertation, Wayne State University, 1965.

Dyer, Calvin O. "Construct Validity of Self-Concept by a Multi-
    trait-Multimethod Analysis." Unpublished Ph.D. Dissertation,
    University of Michigan, 1963.

Engle, Kenneth B. "An Exploratory Study of Significant Others in
    Producing Change in Self-Concept and Achievement in Secondary
    School Underachievers." Unpublished Ed.D. Dissertation,
    Michigan State University, 1964.

Halkides, Galatia. "An Investigation of Therapeutic Success as a
    Function of Therapist Variables." Unpublished Ph.D. Disser-
    tation, University of Chicago, 1958.

Hayes, Edward J. "Relationships Between Self-Concept of Arithmetic
    and Arithmetic Achievement in a Selected Group of Sixth Grade

Students." Unpublished Ph.D. Dissertation, Michigan State University, 1967.

Meyers, Edna O. "Self-Concept, Family Structure and School Achievement: A Study of Disadvantaged Negro Boys." Unpublished Ed.D. Dissertation, Columbia University, 1966.

Mott Institute for Community Improvement. "Presentation to Trustees." Unpublished presentation to the Trustees of the Mott Foundation, March 1, 1968.

Office of Director of Community Schools. "Handbook for Tutors." Mimeographed Handbook, New Haven Public Schools, New Haven, Connecticut, 1967.

Schulman, Jacob. "A Comparison Between Ninth and Twelfth Grade Students on Self-Estimates of Abilities and Objective Scores on the Differential Aptitude Test." Unpublished Ed.D. Dissertation, New York University, 1955.

Seymore, John. "The Relationship of Student Role Concept and Self-Concept of Academic Success and Satisfaction." Unpublished Ed.D. Dissertation, Columbia University, 1963.

Other Sources

Brown versus Board of Education of Topeka, 347 U. S. 403 (1954).

California Test Bureau, *Technical Report on the California Test of Mental Maturity Series*. Monterey, California: California Test Bureau, 1964.

Hamachek, Don E. "Motivation in Learning." A pamphlet in the *What Research Says to the Teacher Series*. Washington, D. C.: Association of Classroom Teachers of the National Education Association, 1968.

Morse, William C. "Administration and Scoring Procedures for Self-Esteem Inventory." A mimeographed copy enclosed in a personal correspondence of January 29, 1968.

National Education Association. *Teacher Aides in Large School Systems: Educational Research Service Circular No. 2.* Washington, D. C.: National Education Association, April, 1967.

Sullivan, Elizabeth T., Willis W. Clark, and Ernest W. Tiegs. *Examiner's Manual: California Short-Form Test of Mental Maturity, Level 1.* Monterey, California: California Test Bureau, 1963.

_____, Willis W. Clark, and Ernest W. Tiegs. *Examiner's Manual: California Short-Form Test of Mental Maturity, Level H.* Monterey, California: California Test Bureau, 1964.

Tiegs, Ernest, and Willis W. Clark. *Manual: California Achievement Tests Complete Battery, Forms W and X, Lower Primary.* Monterey, California: California Test Bureau, 1963.

_____, and Willis W. Clark. *Manual: California Achievement Tests Complete Battery, Forms W and X, Upper Primary.* Monterey, California: California Test Bureau, 1963.

APPENDIX A

TEACHER EVALUATION FORM

Complete the following statements. More than one answer is acceptable.

I. The most noteworthy aspects of the Educational Enrichment Program were: (Explain)

_____

_____

II. Was the Educational Enrichment Program disrupting to your classroom routine?

    (a) Yes   No   (Circle one; if yes, explain below)

    (b) _____

        _____

III. If you answered yes to question number II, what would you do to improve the situation? _____

_____

IV. Do you feel the Educational Enrichment Program assisted the children assigned to it?

    (a) Yes ___ No ___

    (b) Explain the reason for your answer: _____

        _____

V. Your working relationships with the tutors were:

_____

_____

VI. Did the tutorial contacts add to your insight regarding the needs of the children in the program?

    (a) Yes ___ No ___

    (b) If yes, in what way? _____

VII. Your working relationships with the MICI supervisors of the program were: (Check the most descriptive phrases)

(a) Over-informative ___   Informative ___
              Non-informative ___

(b) Contacts: Too frequent ___   Frequent ___
                Infrequent ___

(c) Cooperative ___   Uncooperative ___

(d) How could these relationships have been improved?

_____
_____
_____

VIII. Since you have participated in an experimental tutorial program for the past year and therefore possess invaluable insights regarding the program, what would be your suggestions for a future program of this nature?

_____
_____
_____
_____

IX. Would you, as a teacher, participate in a similar program in the future?

(a) Yes ___   No ___

(b) Explain, if you wish. _____
_____
_____

APPENDIX B

RESPONSES TO THE TEACHER EVALUATION FORM

The Teacher Evaluation Form was developed to assess faculty opinions regarding the effectiveness of enrichment tutoring. Respondents to the form included ten of the 11 participating teachers, the principal and the assistant principal. The form contained nine items. Some of the evaluators related more than one response per item.

Teachers responded to Item I, "The most noteworthy aspects of the Educational Enrichment Program were:", in the following manner:

"Changes in pupils' attitudes."

"Stimulated pupils' interests."

"Increased pupils' confidence or self-concept."

"Increased interests in learning or studies."

"One-to-one relationship."

"Community involvement."

"Assistance to children."

Both administrators indicated that the one-to-one relationship was the most noteworthy aspect of enrichment tutoring. Two teachers did not respond to Item I.

In response to Item II, "Was the Educational Enrichment Program disrupting to your classroom routine?", only one of the ten teachers responded in the affirmative. The following explanations were given for the disruptions:

"All children wanted tutors."

"Some untutored children felt left out."

"Tutors wanted to talk about problems during class time."

The administrators did not respond to this item.

Item III, "If you answered 'yes' to Question II, what would you do to improve the situation?", was answered by the teacher who responded "yes" in the following manner: "Involve tutors in classroom projects--produce plays, etc."

Nine of the ten teachers responded with a "yes" to Item IV, "Do you feel the Educational Enrichment Program assisted the children assigned to it?" One teacher did not respond to the item. Both administrators responded "yes" to the item. The following explanations were given:

"Changes in pupils' attitudes."

"Gave pupils a feeling of importance."

"Improvements in pupils' grades."

"Improved pupils' self-confidence."

"Improvement in pupils' reading."

"More classroom participation."

"Individual attention that can't be given in classrooms."

Item V, "Your working relationships with the tutors were:", was answered by nine teachers and one administrator. Responses included:

"Good."

"Discussions of children's problems and best way to approach their problems."

"Very good, but we needed more time."

"Conferences upon child's return and by telephone."

"Stimulating and encouraging concerning pupils' progress."

"Not very good."

In response to Item VI, "Did the tutorial contacts add to your insights regarding the needs of the children in the program?", six teachers answered "yes" while four answered "no." One administrator responded "yes" and the other gave no response. Those who answered "yes" gave the following explanations:

"Permitted me to determine interests of the child."

"By explaining and discussing the child."

"Helped me understand that his class work was not the most important thing to him and that I needed to establish a friendlier attitude with him."

"Became aware of children's strong points and a greater understanding of their personal problems."

"Assessment of children's needs."

"More awareness on my part of pupils' emotional problems."

Ten teachers and two administrators responded to Item VII, which stated, "Your working relationships with the MICI supervisors of the program were: (Check the descriptive phrases)." Eleven of the twelve respondents reported that the relationships were informative and that contacts were frequent. One of the twelve reported that the relationships were non-informative and that the contacts were infrequent. All reported that the supervisors were cooperative in their relationships. In responding to part (d) of Item VII, "How could these relationships have been improved?", the following responses were given:

"More standardized, make a list of points to cover."

"More social situations with child, teacher, and tutor."

"Presentation of results."

"Released time."

"Not sure they could."

Item VIII, "Since you have participated in an experimental tutorial program for the past year and therefore possess invaluable insights regarding the program, what would be your suggestions for a future program of this nature?", elicited the following responses:

"Release time for conferences."

"Too much paper work."

"Get program underway earlier."

"Recommendations made by teacher of previous year."

"More contact with tutors."

"Group meetings of teachers, pupils, and supervisors."

"Teachers provide a list of pupil needs."

"Tests of pupils' progress."

"Involvement of more pupils."

"More time involvement."

"More males."

"More frequent basis."

In response to Item IX, "Would you, as a teacher, participate in a similar program in the future?", all teachers answered "yes."

The administrators gave no response to this item. Part (b) of
Item IX, "Explain, if you wish," evoked the following explanations:

"I feel the children were helped in many ways."

"I feel it was an excellent program and helped the children
in many ways."

"Very interesting and informative."

"I feel it is every teacher's responsibility to aid in the
educational needs of pupils, and I feel this program has
the qualifications for making this a reality."

"It was very helpful to the pupils who participated in the
program."

"I think this program can help to improve pupils' attitudes
and the individual attention is wonderful and badly needed."

"In spite of the drawbacks I mentioned previously, I feel
there is much worth in program of this type. We need more
males in this capacity--especially Negro males."

APPENDIX C

SELF-ESTEEM INVENTORY

NAME _____ DATE _____

SCHOOL _____ TEACHER _____

GRADE _____ ROOM _____

Please mark each statement in the following way:

If the statement describes how you usually feel, put a check in
the column "LIKE ME." If the statement does not describe how you
usually feel, put a check in the column "UNLIKE ME."

There are no right or wrong answers.

	LIKE ME	UNLIKE ME
EXAMPLE: I'm a hard worker.		
1. I spend a lot of time day-dreaming.		
2. I'm pretty sure of myself.		
3. I often wish I were someone else.		
4. I'm easy to like.		
5. I find it very hard to talk in front of the class.		
6. I wish I were younger.		

		LIKE ME	UNLIKE ME
7.	There are lots of things about myself I'd change if I could.		
8.	I can make up my mind without too much trouble.		
9.	I'm a lot of fun to be with.		
10.	I'm proud of my school work.		
11.	Someone always has to tell me what to do.		
12.	It takes me a long time to get used to anything new.		
13.	I'm sorry for the things I do.		
14.	I'm popular with kids my own age.		
15.	I'm doing the best work that I can.		
16.	I give in very easily.		
17.	I can usually take care of myself.		
18.	I'm pretty happy.		
19.	I would rather play with children younger than I.		
20.	I like to be called on in class.		

	LIKE ME	UNLIKE ME
21. I understand myself.		
22. It's pretty tough to be me.		
23. Things are all mixed up in my life.		
24. Kids usually follow my ideas.		
25. I'm not doing as well in school as I'd like to.		
26. I can make up my mind and stick to it.		
27. I don't really like being a (boy), (girl).		
28. I have a low opinion of myself.		
29. I don't like to be with other people.		
30. I often feel upset in school.		
31. I often feel ashamed of myself.		
32. I'm not as nice looking as most people.		
33. If I have something to say, I usually say it.		
34. Kids pick on me very often.		

	LIKE ME	UNLIKE ME
35. My teacher makes me feel I'm not good enough.		
36. I don't care what happens to me.		
37. I'm a failure.		
38. I get upset easily when I'm scolded.		
39. Most people are better liked than I am.		
40. I often get discouraged in school.		
41. Things usually don't bother me.		
42. I can't be depended upon.		

APPENDIX D

ANALYSIS OF COVARIANCE TABLES
FOR THE STATISTICAL HYPOTHESES

TABLE D1.--Analysis of covariance for composite self-concept
between tutored and non-tutored groups at the second-
grade level controlling for prior composite self-
concept.

Source of Variation	Degrees of Freedom	Sum of Squares	Mean Square	F
Between	1	8.35	8.35	.54
Within	19	291.44	15.34	
Total	20	299.79		

TABLE D2.--Analysis of covariance for self-concept between
tutored and non-tutored groups at the second-grade
level controlling for prior self-concept.

Source of Variation	Degrees of Freedom	Sum of Squares	Mean Square	F
Between	1	4.28	4.28	.65
Within	19	125.87	6.62	
Total	20	130.15		

TABLE D3.--Analysis of covariance for social self-concept between tutored and non-tutored groups at the second-grade level controlling for prior social self-concept.

Source of Variation		Degrees of Freedom	Sum of Squares	Mean Square	F
Between		1	.15	.15	.08
Within		19	37.95	2.00	
	Total	20	38.10		

TABLE D4.--Analysis of covariance for school self-concept between tutored and non-tutored groups at the second-grade level controlling for prior school self-concept.

Source of Variation		Degrees of Freedom	Sum of Squares	Mean Square	F
Between		1	.15	.15	.06
Within		19	44.36	2.33	
	Total	20	44.51		

TABLE D5.--Analysis of covariance for composite self-concept between tutored and non-tutored groups at the third-grade level controlling for prior composite self-concept.

Source of Variation		Degrees of Freedom	Sum of Squares	Mean Square	F
Between		1	1.89	1.89	.14
Within		14	189.57	13.54	
	Total	15	191.46		

TABLE D6.--Analysis of covariance for self-concept between tutored and non-tutored groups at the third-grade level controlling for prior self-concept.

Source of Variation	Degrees of Freedom	Sum of Squares	Mean Square	F
Between	1	18.93	18.93	3.54
Within	14	74.90	5.35	
Total	15	93.83		

TABLE D7.--Analysis of covariance for social self-concept between tutored and non-tutored groups at the third-grade level controlling for prior social self-concept.

Source of Variation	Degrees of Freedom	Sum of Squares	Mean Square	F
Between	1	1.08	1.08	.94
Within	14	15.98	1.14	
Total	15	17.06		

TABLE D8.--Analysis of covariance for school self-concept between tutored and non-tutored groups at the third-grade level controlling for prior school self-concept.

Source of Variation	Degrees of Freedom	Sum of Squares	Mean Square	F
Between	1	3.40	3.40	1.94
Within	14	24.49	1.75	
Total	15	27.89		

TABLE D9.--Analysis of covariance for composite self-concept
between tutored and non-tutored groups at the
fourth-grade level controlling for prior composite
self-concept.

Source of Variation	Degrees of Freedom	Sum of Squares	Mean Square	F
Between	1	2.93	2.93	.10
Within	18	528.09		
Total	19	531.02		

TABLE D10.--Analysis of covariance for self-concept between
tutored and non-tutored groups at the fourth-grade
level controlling for prior self-concept.

Source of Variation	Degrees of Freedom	Sum of Squares	Mean Square	F
Between	1	12.24	12.24	.98
Within	18	224.71	12.48	
Total	19	236.95		

TABLE D11.--Analysis of covariance for social self-concept between
tutored and non-tutored groups at the fourth-grade
level controlling for prior social self-concept.

Source of Variation	Degrees of Freedom	Sum of Squares	Mean Square	F
Between	1	13.81	13.81	4.90*
Within	18	50.74	2.82	
Total	19	64.55		

*Significant at .05 level.

TABLE D12.--Analysis of covariance for school self-concept between
tutored and non-tutored groups at the fourth-grade
level controlling for prior school self-concept.

Source of Variation		Degrees of Freedom	Sum of Squares	Mean Square	F
Between		1	.01	.01	.01
Within		18	36.66	2.04	
	Total	19	36.67		

TABLE D13.--Analysis of covariance for educational achievement
between tutored and non-tutored groups at the second-
grade level controlling for prior educational achievement.

Source of Variation		Degrees of Freedom	Sum of Squares	Mean Square	F
Between		1	4.02	4.02	1.04
Within		19	73.55	3.87	
	Total	20	77.57		

TABLE D14.--Analysis of covariance for reading achievement between
tutored and non-tutored groups at the second-grade
level controlling for prior reading achievement.

Source of Variation		Degrees of Freedom	Sum of Squares	Mean Square	F
Between		1	.61	.61	.12
Within		19	98.24	5.17	
	Total	20	98.85		

TABLE D15.--Analysis of covariance for arithmetic achievement between tutored and non-tutored groups at the second-grade level controlling for prior arithmetic achievement.

Source of Variation		Degrees of Freedom	Sum of Squares	Mean Square	F
Between		1	.00	.00	.00
Within		19	284.64	14.98	
	Total	20	284.64		

TABLE D16.--Analysis of covariance for language achievement between tutored and non-tutored groups at the second-grade level controlling for prior language achievement.

Source of Variation		Degrees of Freedom	Sum of Squares	Mean Square	F
Between		1	37.03	37.03	8.54*
Within		19	82.39	4.34	
	Total	20	119.42		

*Significant at .05 level

TABLE D17.--Analysis of covariance for educational achievement between tutored and non-tutored groups at the third-grade level controlling for prior educational achievement.

Source of Variation		Degrees of Freedom	Sum of Squares	Mean Square	F
Between		1	5.24	5.24	1.16
Within		14	63.17	4.51	
	Total	15	68.41		

TABLE D18.--Analysis of covariance for reading achievement
         between tutored and non-tutored groups at the third-
         grade level controlling for prior reading achievement.

Source of Variation	Degrees of Freedom	Sum of Squares	Mean Square	F
Between	1	23.95	23.95	2.63
Within	14	127.42	9.10	
Total	15	151.37		

TABLE D19.--Analysis of covariance for arithmetic achievement
         between tutored and non-tutored groups at the third-
         grade level controlling for prior arithmetic achieve-
         ment.

Source of Variation	Degrees of Freedom	Sum of Squares	Mean Square	F
Between	1	40.37	40.37	5.46*
Within	14	103.43	7.39	
Total	15	143.80		

*Significant at .05 level.

TABLE D20.--Analysis of covariance for language achievement
         between tutored and non-tutored groups at the third-
         grade level controlling for prior language achievement.

Source of Variation	Degrees of Freedom	Sum of Squares	Mean Square	F
Between	1	.64	.64	.04
Within	14	245.82	17.56	
Total	15	246.46		

TABLE D21.--Analysis of covariance for educational achievement between tutored and non-tutored groups at the fourth-grade level controlling for prior educational achievement.

Source of Variation		Degrees of Freedom	Sum of Squares	Mean Square	F
Between		1	3.87	3.87	.55
Within		18	126.16	7.01	
	Total	19	130.03		

TABLE D22.--Analysis of covariance for reading achievement between tutored and non-tutored groups at the fourth-grade level controlling for prior reading achievement.

Source of Variation		Degrees of Freedom	Sum of Squares	Mean Square	F
Between		1	10.17	10.17	.98
Within		18	187.45	10.41	
	Total	19	197.62		

TABLE D23.--Analysis of covariance for arithmetic achievement between tutored and non-tutored groups at the fourth-grade level controlling for prior arithmetic achievement.

Source of Variation		Degrees of Freedom	Sum of Squares	Mean Square	F
Between		1	20.46	20.46	1.15
Within		18	319.86	17.77	
	Total	19	340.32		

TABLE D24.--Analysis of covariance for language achievement
            between tutored and non-tutored groups at the fourth-
            grade level controlling for prior language achievement.

Source of Variation		Degrees of Freedom	Sum of Squares	Mean Square	F
Between		1	4.98	4.98	.19
Within		18	466.99	25.94	
	Total	19	471.97		

TABLE D25.--Analysis of covariance for measured intelligence
            between tutored and non-tutored groups at the second-
            grade level controlling for prior measured intelli-
            gence.

Source of Variation		Degrees of Freedom	Sum of Squares	Mean Square	F
Between		1	24.52	24.52	.50
Within		19	928.64	48.88	
	Total	20	953.16		

TABLE D26.--Analysis of covariance for language intelligence
            between tutored and non-tutored groups at the second-
            grade level controlling for prior language intelli-
            gence.

Source of Variation		Degrees of Freedom	Sum of Squares	Mean Square	F
Between		1	45.31	45.31	1.05
Within		19	822.21	43.27	
	Total	20	867.52		

TABLE D27.--Analysis of covariance for non-language intelligence
between tutored and non-tutored groups at the
second-grade level controlling for prior non-language
intelligence.

Source of Variation		Degrees of Freedom	Sum of Squares	Mean Square	F
Between		1	4.85	4.85	.05
Within		19	1919.96	101.05	
	Total	20	1924.81		

TABLE D28.--Analysis of covariance for measured intelligence
between tutored and non-tutored groups at the third-
grade level controlling for prior measured intelligence.

Source of Variation		Degrees of Freedom	Sum of Squares	Mean Square	F
Between		1	.16	.16	.00
Within		14	755.63	53.97	
	Total	15	755.79		

TABLE D29.--Analysis of covariance for language intelligence
between tutored and non-tutored groups at the third-
grade level controlling for prior language intelligence.

Source of Variation		Degrees of Freedom	Sum of Squares	Mean Square	F
Between		1	94.02	94.02	2.29
Within		14	574.13	41.01	
	Total	15	668.15		

TABLE D30.--Analysis of covariance for non-language intelligence
between tutored and non-tutored groups at the third-
grade level controlling for prior non-language intelligence

Source of Variation		Degrees of Freedom	Sum of Squares	Mean Square	F
Between		1	28.77	28.77	.36
Within		14	1126.77	80.48	
	Total	15	1155.54		

TABLE D31.--Analysis of covariance for measured intelligence
between tutored and non-tutored groups at the fourth-
grade level controlling for prior measured intelligence.

Source of Variation		Degrees of Freedom	Sum of Squares	Mean Square	F
Between		1	66.53	66.53	.38
Within		18	3148.17	174.90	
	Total	19	3214.70		

TABLE D32.--Analysis of covariance for language intelligence
between tutored and non-tutored groups at the fourth-
grade level controlling for prior language intelligence.

Source of Variation		Degrees of Freedom	Sum of Squares	Mean Square	F
Between		1	43.07	43.07	.26
Within		18	2927.62	162.65	
	Total	19	2970.69		

TABLE D33.--Analysis of covariance for non-language intelligence between tutored and non-tutored groups at the fourth-grade level controlling for prior non-language intelligence.

Source of Variation		Degrees of Freedom	Sum of Squares	Mean Square	F
Between		1	175.58	175.58	1.05
Within		18	2997.89	166.55	
	Total	19	3173.47		